SURVIVING BULLIES,

QUEEN BEES & PSYCHOPATHS

IN THE WORKPLACE

by Patricia G. Barnes, J.D.

barnespatg@gmail.com

http://abusergoestowork.com/

Paperback ISBN 978-0-615-64241-3

E-book ISBN: 978-0-9898708-6-3

Many thanks to:

Cover Design by **Doren Chapman**

Copy Editor **John (Gene) Michals**

Technical assistance from John **E. Barnes-McKivigan**

To employers who respect
the worth and dignity
of the human beings
who toil in their enterprise

Table of Contents

1. THE PROBLEM

"Many who live with violence day in and day out assume it is an intrinsic part of the human condition. But this is not so. Violence can be prevented. Violent cultures can be turned around ... Governments, communities and individuals can make a difference." Nelson Mandela

Workplace bullying is epidemic in America, and it is getting worse as our economic travails leave workers with fewer employment options, less job security, and more vulnerable to abuse.

I became interested in workplace bullying while employed at a domestic violence organization, one that paradoxically suffered from a bullying culture. Management, which included mostly women who had worked in the domestic violence field for years, used tactics that were not unlike those that abusers use in intimate-partner relationships. Tactics like berating or humiliating subordinates, making unreasonable demands and threats, shunning employees, etc. Sometimes bullies are bona-fide psychopaths but I suspect these supervisors were simply modeling management techniques they endured as underlings early in their careers.

Like most organizations, managers in this workplace were not promoted because they had the skills necessary to be a good manager, but because someone abruptly resigned, leaving a vacancy. Or they were good at something that had nothing to do with management, such as the ability to track budgetary numbers, create educational materials, or organize conferences. And they received little or virtually no management training.

But the result was nine hours or more, per workday, of an emotionally toxic environment. A workplace riddled with irrationality and fear. And every six months or so, another target of bullying, finally fed up or dry-gulched by a senior manager, walked down the hallway to the elevator, toting her meager possessions in a cardboard box.

Consider:

- A scientific CareerBuilder survey in 2011 found that one in four workers (27 percent) is bullied.

- A 2010 scientific poll by Zogby International for the Workplace Bullying Institute of Bellingham, WA, showed that 37 percent of employees are bullied at the workplace – that's 54 million workers!

- A 2007 scientific poll by the Employment Law Alliance found that nearly 45 percent of workers worked for an abusive boss or employer at some point in their career.

- A 2004 survey by the National Institute for Occupational Safety and Health (NIOSH) found that,

"24.5% of the companies surveyed reported that some degree of bullying had occurred there during the preceding year."

- A leading psychologist on workplace abuse examined fifteen psychological studies; most reported that at least half of workers experienced "emotional abuse" on the job. (See Loraleigh Keashly, *Emotional Abuse in the Workplace: Conceptual and Empirical Issues*, 1 J. Emotional Abuse 85, 114 (1998))

Note: One reason for conflicting data is that there is no uniformly accepted definition of bullying.

Clearly, a significant percentage of Americans experience the workplace as a hostile and abusive place – a place where workplace violence is rampant.

Workplace bullying is widely recognized as a form of workplace violence. The International Labour Organization says workplace bullying is one of the fastest growing forms of workplace violence. According to NIOSH:

Workplace violence is any physical assault, threatening behavior or verbal abuse occurring in the work setting. It includes but is not limited to beatings, stabbing, suicides, shootings, rapes, near suicides, psychological traumas such as threats, obscene phone calls, an intimidating presence, and harassment of any nature such as being followed, sworn at or shouted at.

Similarly, the U.S. Department of Justice (DOJ) in 2003 defined workplace violence as "any form of conduct that intentionally creates anxiety, fear and a climate of distrust in the workplace." The types of workplace violence recognized by the DOJ range from homicide and rape to sexual harassment and physical/emotional abuse and bullying.

Workplace bullying is not about normal workplace conflict, petty slights, or rude behavior. Bullying can be the equivalent of a thousand pin pricks that results in a mortal wound. It involves systematic and repetitive harassment over a period of time. Typically, it continues until the target is demoted, fired or forced to quit. Bullying is an intentional abuse of power, usually by a boss, sometimes by a group of "mobbing" co-workers.

To differentiate workplace bullying from normal workplace conflict, experts have created a new vocabulary that emphasizes the intentional and violent nature of the problem. Victims are called targets - to emphasize that they are singled out for abusive treatment by a bully. The mental and physical harms that targets suffer are referred to as injuries, to focus attention on the bully who has intentionally caused the injuries. In recent years, a new term has entered the American lexicon – bullycide –which refers to an individual who becomes depressed over bullying and commits suicide.

Illegal but...

Workplace bullying causes targets to suffer potentially severe psychological and physical harm. For that reason, it arguably is illegal. The Occupational Safety and Health Act's (OSH Act), General Duty Clause, Section 5(a)(1) §5, requires employers to provide workers with a workplace free from recognized hazards that are likely to cause or are causing death or serious physical harm. There is an enormous body of research showing that targets of workplace bullying suffer from depression, stress and anxiety, insomnia, and that workplace stress contributes to chronic disease including cardiovascular disease and an impaired immune system.

Many other countries have treated workplace bullying as an important health and safety issue for years. Ireland's Health and Safety Authority adopted a *Code of Practice for Employers and Employees on the Prevention and Resolution of Bullying at Work* in 2007 that requires employers to "prevent, so far as is reasonably practicable, any improper conduct or behaviour likely to put the safety, health and welfare at work of his or her employees at risk."

The European Union in 2000 adopted *The Charter of the Fundamental Rights of the European Union* (EU), which declares that "every worker has the right to working conditions which respect his or her health, safety and dignity." Europe's leading business and labor organizations signed *The European Framework Agreement on Harassment and Violence at Work* in 2007. The agreement states that employers have a duty to protect workers from harassment and violence in the workplace.

France in 2002 adopted a law against "moral harassment" and Belgium passed a law equating bullying with harassment. Courts in the United Kingdom ruled the 1997 Protection from Harassment Act encompasses the workplace and makes it a criminal offence to harass a person. Several Canadian provinces have passed workplace bully laws, as have Queensland and Victoria, Australia. In Germany, courts and labor unions have addressed the problem.

Sweden was the first country to adopt a workplace bullying law in 1993. Sweden requires employers to organize the workplace with the goal of preventing bullying, to adopt policies to detect and immediately respond to bullying, and to provide support to targets of bullying. The Swedish National Board of Occupational Safety and Health defines victimization as "recurrent, reprehensible or distinctly negative actions…directed against individual employees in an offensive manner and can result in those employees being placed outside the workplace community." Sweden's law is in response to the work of Dr. Heinz Leymann, an industrial psychologist who began studying workplace bullying in Sweden the early 1980s. Leymann referred to workplace bullying as "mobbing," a term derived from a natural phenomenon in which members of a bird or animal species band together to expel a disfavored member of the group.

Despite international recognition of workplace bullying, efforts to address the problem in the United States - ongoing since at least 2002 - thus far have failed. The U.S. Occupational Health and Safety Administration (OSHA) has ignored workplace bullying as a national issue. Grassroots efforts to pass state legislation to stop workplace bullying over the past decade has yet to yield a single victory. Even if one state does pass a workplace anti-bullying law, it will take decades (if ever) for all states to do so.

The High Cost

Why do the U.S. government and so many American employers tolerate workplace bullying, even while governments and employers in other countries do not? Bullying may be the single most preventable and needless expense on any company's business ledger.

For one thing, bullying invites litigation. Bullying is an underlying factor in many lawsuits alleging discrimination and wrongful termination. One study found evidence of a relationship between general incivility, gender-related harassment, and sexual harassment. The study concluded that sexual harassment occurs "against a backdrop of generalized disrespect in the workplace." (See S. Lim & L.M. Cortina, *Interpersonal mistreatment in the workplace: The interface and impact of general incivility and sexual harassment*, 90 Journal of Applied Psychology, 483-

496(2005)). An employer can easily spend more than $100,000 to defend even a meritless lawsuit.

Of course, plaintiffs don't always lose in court. The Indiana Supreme Court in 2008 upheld a jury award of $325,000 to an Indiana medical technical who was bullied by a surgeon in a hospital operating room. The jury found that the technician was the victim of assault because he was placed in imminent fear of bodily harm by the surgeon, even though the surgeon never physically touched him. (See *Raess v. Doescher*, 883 N.E.2d 790 (2008)).

Employers also pay for bullying in terms of reduced productivity, unnecessary turnover, absenteeism, higher health care premiums and greater workers' compensation costs. Bullying is estimated to cost billions each year.

Bullies often select targets who are highly competent, accomplished and popular employees. Bullies see these workers as a threat. An employer can lose its best employees to bullying. And that's not all. Co-workers who witness bullying behaviors also suffer stress. They often "play it safe" so they won't be next in the line of fire. They may start circulating *their* resumes. After targets and witnesses of bullying leave their jobs, they frequently bad-mouth the employer, driving away potential customers and deterring future recruitment of quality new employees. Of all of a company's assets, its reputation is arguably the most important - and the easiest to lose.

Estimates for the cost of bullying to American employers range from $64 billion to more than $300 billion.

Society collectively incurs losses from workplace bullying in the form of reduced productivity, increased health and social welfare costs, disability payments etc. Workers who lose their jobs may face eviction, foreclosure and homelessness. They apply for unemployment compensation and food stamps. They show up in hospital emergency rooms because they lost their medical insurance and were unable to treat an illness in the early stages. And the list goes on.

Considering the cost that bullying exacts on society, employers and employees, America's failure to address workplace bullying as a national problem is baffling.

Bad Companies

One reason that workplace bullying is tolerated in the United States may involve the nature of bullying itself. We often think of workplace bullies as maladjusted individuals. The problem, however, is not always with individuals. Workplace bullying also is used intentionally by unscrupulous employers to achieve organizational goals, such as to boost short-term production, downsize without paying unemployment benefits, or to get rid employees who are "troublemakers" (demanding legal rights, fair pay, overtime, etc.). Deliberate bullying by employers is called "strategic harassment."

Such appeared to be the case in 2011 when a federal judge in Pennsylvania refused to dismiss a worker's claim of discrimination filed under the Americans with Disabilities Act. The case involved a technician at a surgical training center who was fired a few hours after telling his boss that he had a condition that required hip replacement surgery. (See Linhart *v. Zitelli & Broadland, P.C.,* W.D. PA (10/19/11)) The judge rejected the employer's defense that the worker was fired for performance reasons. The Court questioned the defendant's credibility and said the plaintiff had raised a reasonable inference of discrimination because of the timing of his dismissal.

Sometimes strategic harassment can be addressed legally through a retaliation claim if federal or state statutes provide for such a claim. Even then, however, employers know that many workers do not understand their rights, lack the time or ability to enforce their rights, and, even if they wanted to act, cannot find an attorney to help them navigate the court system.

I routinely encountered victims of workplace bullying while working briefly as an attorney on class-action lawsuits charging that employers failed to pay legal wages and overtime as required under the Fair Labor Standards Act. I discovered that blue-collar workers often are bullied after they complain they were "shorted" on overtime pay or benefits.

In one case, a young Hispanic forklift operator, a first-generation American, complained to HR that he was not paid earned overtime for several weeks in a row. The next day, he said, his immediate supervisor, his former mentor, began a campaign of unrelenting harassment. After a few months of constant ridicule and humiliation, the forklift operator said he quit because he feared he would otherwise suffer a nervous breakdown. This young man quickly went from being a middle class worker with a wife and two young children to a divorced man living in his car. It was expected that he and other class members would potentially collect a few thousand dollars in damages for the lost overtime.

American employers who automatically decry proposed legislation to address workplace bullying often express concerns about the costs and frivolous lawsuits. But it is not inconceivable that some employers also want to preserve their "right" to engage in strategic harassment.

Poor Management

Even if workplace bullying is unintentional, it usually reflects poor management practices. A bullying culture often is an indicator of structural problems within a company that involve power and inequity - problems that can only be resolved at the organizational level. (See Jamie L. Callahan, *Incivility as an Instrument of Oppression: Exploring the Role of Power in Constructions of Civility* Advances in Developing Human Resources 13(1) 10–21 (2011)) Employers can encourage bullying through autocratic leadership, overloading employees with excessive work, role confusion, a blame culture, setting unattainable goals, or encouraging intense competition among co-workers. If the employer ignores or denies conflict or fails to deal with it effectively, the bullying worsens.

It stands to reason that only employers can stop bullying. If an employer refuses to tolerate bullying in the workplace, it will stop. Employees, especially those who are non-unionized, lack the power to address and stop bullying which roots in the organization itself.

Some employers are complacent about bullying due to ignorance. Small businesses often grow without professional managers, while mid-to-large size employers may not train managers to deal with conflict. An international study found that fewer than half of managers receive any training in workplace conflict. (*CPP Global Human Capital Report*, 4 (June 2009)). Employers may not understand the difference between a tough-but-fair boss and a bully boss who acts for personal reasons that often are contrary to the employer's best interests.

In the final analysis, however, it is irrelevant whether an employer is ignorant about the harm caused by bullying. A hallowed pillar of American jurisprudence is *ignorantia juris non excusat or ignorantia legis neminem excusat* - ignorance of the law excuses no one.

Stopping It

Some countries, such as Sweden and Spain, view workplace bullying from a health and safety perspective. They use regulatory laws – like the U.S. Occupational Health and Safety Act (OSH Act) - to require employers to protect employees from workplace bullying, just as these laws protect workers from exposure to toxic chemicals or other workplace hazards.

Alternatively, workplace bullying may be viewed as a type of abuse that results in a hostile working environment.

The Workplace Bullying Institute has spearheaded a grassroots effort for more than a decade to pass workplace anti-bully legislation on a state-by-state basis. The Institute supports passage of the proposed Healthy Workplace Bill, which has been considered by about two dozen states. As of 2012, no state had adopted the proposed bill, even though it is far less protective than similar legislation in other countries. Meanwhile, a Nevada legislator, Richard "Tick" Segerblom, a Las Vegas employment lawyer, twice proposed addressing workplace bullying by expanding the scope of the Nevada law that is patterned after the leading federal anti-discrimination law (Title VII of the Civil Rights Act). Segerblom's proposed bill would allow any employee who is the victim of a hostile workplace environment to file suit, not just employees who now have protected status (i.e., race, sex, age, etc.) under Title VII.

13

I have co-launched a petition drive asking the U.S. President and Secretary of Labor to formulate a uniform, national response to the problem of workplace bullying. (See, http://www.thepetitionsite.com/1/protect-us-workers/)

Without a law that specifically addresses bullying, targets must look to a hodgepodge of existing federal and state laws that govern discrimination, contract law and tort or personal injury law. Much of workplace bullying falls outside existing laws but certainly not all of it. Discrimination complaints are the most common types of workplace litigation, and it is easy to see how bullying can factor into a discrimination complaint.

Consider Ashley Alford, 21, who worked at one of 1,800 stores operated by the rent-to-own company, The Aaron's, Inc.

Shortly after Alford began working as a customer service representative at an Aaron's store in Illinois in 2005, she became a victim of sexual harassment by the store's then-general manager, Richard Moore. It started with crude sexual jokes but ended in an assault. Alford said Moore sneaked up behind her in the fall of 2006 as she was sitting on the floor of the stockroom and hit her on the head with his penis. In another incident, Moore allegedly threw Alford to the ground, lifted her shirt and masturbated over her as he held her down. Alford called a company harassment hotline to no avail. Then Moore's supervisor allegedly confronted Ashford - in front of Moore - and warned Moore to "watch his back" because of Ashford's complaint.

A federal jury in 2011 ordered Aaron's to pay Ashford a whopping $95 million in damages. The jury found that Moore had assaulted and battered Alford. It said Aaron's was liable for negligent supervision, sexual harassment and Intentional Infliction of Emotional Distress. The judge subsequently lowered the sexual harassment part of the jury award from $45 million to $300,000 (pursuant to a statutory cap) but Aaron's was still on the hook for more than $40 million, plus attorney fees. Aaron's entire profit in 2010 was $118 million.

Ashford's case includes an assortment of claims but it boils down to a supervisor who felt entitled to bully and abuse a young woman subordinate, and a company that was complacent about the problem.

The Equal Employment Opportunities Commission (EEOC) reports that private sector workplace discrimination filings hit an unprecedented high - 99,922 - during the fiscal year ending Sept. 30, 2010. For the first time, the EEOC said, retaliation complaints (36,258) outnumbered race discrimination complaints (35,890). Other types of workplace suits involved discrimination on the basis of sex (29,029), disability (25,165), age (23,264), national origin (11,304) and religion (3,790). All of these lawsuits cost U.S. businesses – and society in general – time, money and resources. And many of these lawsuits might have been avoided if the employer had put in place reasonable policies to prevent and stop workplace bullying.

This book will explore legal considerations pertaining to workplace bullying and the state of the law.

Employees should read this book because it explains workplace bullying and provides a roadmap for how to respond effectively to the problem. If everything else fails, targets and/or their attorneys can review the array of federal and state laws discussed in this book to ascertain whether there is a potential legal cause of action.

At present, no federal or state law prohibits workplace bullying and many courts see bullying as part of a normal job environment. Therefore, the legal tools described in this book will not offer every target with a just solution. At the same time, the most important survival tool may not be legal in nature; it may simply be the recognition by targets that what they are or have experienced constitutes workplace bullying. Targets do not suddenly become incompetent, inept or otherwise unemployable. Targets are singled out for abuse and mistreatment by bullies. Recognizing the signs and common patterns of abuse can help targets make sense of a workplace that suddenly has become irrational and toxic.

This book will help employers recognize the problem of workplace bullying - and to act proactively to limit their risk. Workplace bullying is like a cancer in an organization, disrupting normal business operations and eroding profits. Bullies are concerned primarily with their personal desire for power and control and not about the company's best interests. Like the Ghost of Christmas Future, this book foretells of the potentially dire consequences that can result from complacency about bullying in the workplace.

Of course, nothing in this book should be construed as legal advice, which is only appropriate after a thorough review of the facts of a specific case.

Psychopath in the Corner Office?

"Chainsaw" Al Dunlap became notorious during the era of unabashed greed on Wall Street in the 1990s. But was he a psychopath?

In his 18 months as chief executive of Scott Paper Co., then the world's leading tissue producer, Dunlap fired 11,000 employees. He cut all corporate philanthropy and slashed expenditures on planned improvements and research. Dunlap sold Scott, which was founded in 1897, to its arch-rival, Kimberly Paper Corp, in 1995.

Scott Paper Co. was the sixth company that Dunlap had sold or dismembered since 1983.

Executives recalled sessions where Dunlap verbally assaulted them for hours, terrifying them with threats of dismissal. "You couldn't look the guy in the eye for fear you would get fired or at least dressed down for no reason at all," said one worker.

Dunlop was so hated that he supposedly wore a bulletproof vest and carried a handgun.

Journalist Jon Ronson, author of a 2011 book, *The Psychopath Test,* interviewed Dunlap to see if he fit the criteria of psychopath set forth in the 20-item Robert Hare Psychopathy Checklist. A psychopath is characterized primarily by a lack of empathy and remorse, shallow emotions, egocentricity, and deceptiveness.

Ronson said Dunlop admitted to possessing many traits of a psychopath but Dunlop re-cast those traits positively.

- Inability to feel a deep range of emotion? "Why get weighed down by emotions?"

- A grandiose sense of self worth? "Believe in yourself!"

- Manipulative? "I describe that as leadership, getting people to do what you want them to."

Ronson estimates the incidence of psychopathy among corporate chief executive officers is about 4 percent, which is four times what it is in the population at large. However, he concluded Dunlap was not an actual psychopath because Dunlap lacked at least a couple of traits of a psychopath. For example, Ronson said, Dunlap had no record of juvenile delinquency and he was in a long-standing marriage.

Along the same lines, a former British academic, Clive R. Boddy, advanced a theory in his 2011 book, *Corporate Psychopaths: Organizational Destroyers,* that the worldwide global financial meltdown was largely the fault of corporate psychopaths at the helm of financial institutions on Wall Street.

Boddy writes that psychopaths are the one percent of "people who - perhaps due to physical factors having to do with abnormal brain connectivity and chemistry" - lack a "conscience, have few emotions and display an inability to have any feelings, sympathy or empathy for other people." Psychopaths, writes Boddy, are "extraordinarily cold, much more calculating and ruthless towards others than most people are and therefore a menace to the companies they work for and to society."

2. WHAT'S REALLY AT STAKE?

'From the depth of need and despair, people can work together, can organize themselves to solve their own problems and fill their own needs with dignity and strength." - *Cesar Chavez*

Health Hazards

Testifying at a March 2011 hearing of the Maryland General Assembly in support of a workplace anti-bullying bill, Kathie Gant said she worked as an administrative assistant to a Maryland attorney who terrorized her for a year – causing her mental and emotional trauma. The woman denigrated her in front of peers, threw pencils at her (because she wanted them sharper), and closed a door locking Gant inside a dark storage closet. Gant said she complained twice to Human Resources. The first HR representative suggested that she quit the job she had held for a decade; the second one referred her to the company's Employment Assistance Program (EAP). After months of abuse, Gant had lost 20 pounds and wasn't sleeping. An EAP therapist referred Gant to a psychiatrist, who said she was suffering from extreme anxiety and depression and recommended hospitalization

It takes surprisingly little time – just a few weeks or months -- for workplace bullies to inflict serious mental and physical damage upon their targets. More than the cost to society and employers, the real tragedy of workplace bullying is the human toll.

Some workers who are bullied experience constant fear of attack, which can compromise the body's ability to repair and defend itself, leading to short term and long term physical health problems. The U.S. Department of Health's Centers for Disease Control (CDC), says stress sets off an alarm in the brain, which responds by preparing the body for defensive action. The nervous system is aroused and hormones are released to sharpen the senses, quicken the pulse, deepen respiration, and tense the muscles. This response, called the "fight or flight" response, is preprogrammed biologically. And everyone responds pretty much in the same way.

The CDC says studies in the past 20 years have found a relationship between job stress and common ailments like mood and sleep disturbances, upset stomach and headache. The CDC says evidence is rapidly accumulating to suggest that stress over the long term plays an important role in chronic health problems, including, musculoskeletal disorders, psychological disorders, and cardiovascular diseases (the leading cause of death in the United States).

The apparent relationship between job stress and cardiovascular disease is particularly troubling in the context of workplace bullying. The Center for the Promotion of Health in the

New England Workplace estimates that up to 23 percent of heart disease related deaths per year could be prevented if work-related strain in the most stressful occupations were reduced to average levels seen in other occupations. The center says effective ways to reduce stress in the workplace include clarifying worker roles, improving worker-management communication, and ensuring a "respectful work environment."

A bad boss can seriously affect a worker's health. Anna Nyberg at the Stress Institute in Stockholm led a research team in Sweden that studied more than 3,100 men for more than a decade in typical work settings. In a 2008 article in the Journal of Occupational and Environmental Medicine, she reported that employees who had managers who were incompetent, inconsiderate, secretive and uncommunicative were 60 percent more likely than other employees to experience a heart attack or life-threatening cardiac condition. Meanwhile, employees who worked with "good" leaders were 40 percent less likely than other employees to suffer heart problems. Nyberg says the study confirms that employees who work for managers who "behave strangely, or in any way they don't understand" feel stress that develops into a health risk.

If an inconsiderate boss is a health hazard, imagine working for a bully boss! English psychologist Dr. Noreen Tehrani says bullied workers go through the same emotions and stress as battle-scarred soldiers returning from combat overseas. In her 2004 study of 165 nurses and social workers, she said 36 percent of the men and 42 percent of the women reported having been bullied. She said that one in five of the bullied workers exhibited the main symptoms of Post Traumatic Stress Disorder (PTSD), including hyper arousal, a feeling of constant anxiety and over-vigilance and avoidance of factors related to the traumatizing event. PTSD also is characterized by repeated and painful reliving of the event in the form of dreams, flashbacks and intense distress whenever exposed to reminders.

"The symptoms displayed by people who have been in conflict situations and workplaces where bullying happens are strikingly similar," says Dr Tehrani. "Both groups suffer nightmares, are jumpy, and seem fueled by too much adrenaline …. In addition, they show greater susceptibility to illnesses, heart disease and alcoholism."

The American Psychological Association reported in 2011 that the nation may be "on the verge of a stress-induced public health crisis." In, *Stress in America: Our Health at Risk,* the APA surveyed 1.226 U.S. residents, of whom 22 percent reported extreme stress. Money (75%), work (70%) and the economy (67%) were the most frequently cited causes of stress for Americans. The APA also found that participants rely on unhealthy sedentary behaviors to manage this stress – eating, television viewing, listening to music, etc. According to the APA report, 33.8 percent of American adults are obese and one in ten suffers from depression -- conditions that are exacerbated by stress.

Various studies show that stress is a "major driver of chronic illness, which in turn is a major driver of escalating health care costs in this country," says APA Chief Executive Officer Norman B. Anderson, Ph.D. "It is critical that the entire health community and policymakers recognize the role of stress and unhealthy behaviors in causing and exacerbating chronic health conditions, and support models of care that help people make positive changes."

A study of workplace conflict in nine countries found that a quarter of workers said workplace conflict made them sick or caused them to be absent from work. The study estimates that employees spend an average of 2.1 hours a week dealing with non-productive conflict, costing employers billions. (CPP Global Human Capital Report, June 2009).

Research suggests that general workplace bullying is more harmful to employees than sexual harassment. Researchers at the University of Manitoba reviewed 110 studies -- conducted over 21 years -- and compared employees' experience of sexual harassment with other forms of workplace aggression. They determined that workplace bullying had more-severe consequences than sexual harassment, with bullied workers reporting more job stress and higher levels of anger and anxiety. The researchers said bullying may be more harmful because it is more insidious, difficult to report, and carries no sanction. (See M. Sandy Hershcovis & Julian Barling, *Comparing the Outcomes of Sexual Harassment and Workplace Aggression: A Meta-Analysis*, presented at the Seventh Annual Work, Stress, & Health Conference, Washington, D.C. (2008)).

Risk to Family

Workplace bullying can be so intense that it migrates from the office to the home front, where it impacts the well-being of the worker's family.

A 2001 study in Denmark found that workplace bullying can damage many other aspects of a target's life. Almost three-quarters of the targets surveyed reported that the bullying led to impaired relationships with friends and family and diminished leisure, household, and sexual activities. (*See* E. Mikkelson, & S. Einarsen, *Bullying in Danish work-life: Prevalence and health correlates*, 10 European Journal of Work and Organizational Psychology, 393–414 (2001)).

Stress suffered by targets of workplace abuse may result in a shift of family responsibilities to the target's partner, according to Professor Merideth J. Ferguson, PhD., an assistant professor of management and entrepreneurship at the Baylor University Hankamer School of Business conducted a study in 2011. She said these increased demands may interfere with the partner's work life.

Ferguson's study also found that stress from bullying significantly affects the target and his or her partner's marital satisfaction. "This research underlines the importance of stopping incivility before it starts so that the ripple effect of incivility does not impact the employee's family and potentially inflict further damage beyond the workplace ... and cross over into the workplace of the partner," said Ferguson.

Ferguson advised targets of bullying to seek support through their company's employee assistance program, or otherwise obtain counseling or stress management to identify tactics or mechanisms to buffer the impact of incivility on the family

Bullycide

There are many reported cases of students and workers who committed suicide after being bullied. So many that in recent years these individuals have been called victims of "bullycide."

Yale University researchers in 2008 analyzed 37 studies in various countries that examined bullying and suicide among children and adolescents. The researchers concluded that almost all of the studies found connections between bullying and suicidal thoughts among children. Five studies reported that bullying victims were two to nine times more likely to report suicidal thoughts than other children were. The studies took place in the United States, Canada, several European countries (including the United Kingdom and Germany), South Korea, Japan and South Africa. (See Young Shin Kim, MD, MS, MPH, PhD and Bennett

26

Leventhal, MD, *Bullying and Suicide: A Review*, 20(2) Int. J Adolesc. Med Health 133-154 (2008)).

It seems logical that bullying also would affect the thoughts of adults in the workplace. At least one study shows that major depressive disorder—often with suicidal ideation—is frequently associated with being bullied in the workplace. (Girardi P, Monaco E, Prestigiacomo C, et al. *Personality and Psychopathological Profiles in Individuals Exposed to Mobbing,* 22 Violence and Victims, 172-188 (2007).

Adults depend upon a paycheck for their economic survival and that of their families. A large part of many adults' self-identity and self-worth is linked to their work. Being fired or terminated from a position can be a devastating blow to anyone. Imagine having your self-esteem eviscerated by a bully for months and then being handed a pink slip.

A pioneer in the study of workplace bullying, Heinz Leymann, an occupational psychologist, estimated in 1990 that between 10 percent and 15 percent of all suicides in Sweden each year were directly related to workplace mobbing. (Heinz Leymann, *Mobbing and Psychological Terror at Workplaces*, 5 Violence and Victims, 119-125 (1990)).

Several suicides in the United States in recent years have been linked to alleged workplace bullying. Little research has been done in this area and there are inherent difficulties in assigning blame and attributing causation in such complex matters. Moral questions raised by these cases are subject to interpretation, leaving a messy gray area regarding the responsibility of the alleged bully for the suicide. Still, it seems almost intuitive that workplace bullying is at least a factor in workplace suicides.

Katherine Hermes, a history professor, told a committee of the Connecticut legislature that workplace bullying led to the 2005 suicide of her friend, Marlene A. Braun, 46, the first manager of the Carrizo Plain National Monument Santa Margarita, CA. Braun left a note stating that her boss had made her life "utterly unbearable" and that she "could no longer take (his) abuse, humiliation and lies."

Dr. Hermes said Braun's journal contained a chronology of her last year, including descriptions of when her boss allegedly screamed at her and then suspended her out of the blue. The suspension was the first black mark in Braun's 13-year career in government service. After a contentious meeting about cattle grazing rights at the monument site, Braun said that her boss blocked her car on a narrow road with his truck, got out, and threatened her, telling her she had "brought this" on herself.

According to Dr. Hermes, Braun became depressed and lost 40 pounds in little over a year. Braun requested a medical leave and presented her boss with a doctor's note. Even though Braun had never previously requested a leave, Hermes said, Braun's boss insisted that she fill out a long form used for employees who abuse the sick leave policy. "He saw what was happening to her and he did not care," said Dr. Hermes.

A subsequent investigation by an Inspector General for the U.S. Department of the Interior absolved Braun's supervisor -- and the Bakersfield, CA, office of the U.S. Bureau of Land Management's (BLM) -- of blame in Braun's death. At the same time, the Inspector General faulted Braun's boss for failing to adequately resolve personal and professional conflicts, and concluded that the BLM "did not take action to resolve long-standing differences" or to defuse interoffice conflict "despite the availability of alternative dispute resolution methods."

Similarly, the University of Virginia concluded it was not responsible for the 2010 suicide of the Kevin Morrissey, 52, the managing editor of the prestigious Virginia Quarterly Review (VQR). Morrissey's sister and co-workers said Morrissey had endured weeks of abuse and harassment from his boss, VQR Editor Ted Genoways. Morrissey complained several times to university administrators in the weeks prior to his death. In a July 26, 2010 email to UV's Chief of Staff, Morrissey wrote:

> "The communication difficulties between Ted and myself have been going on for over three years at this point, and I feel I have made a concerted and conscientious effort to follow through on all UVA prescribed methods for dealing with the issue. I've spoken numerous times to Ted, without gaining a satisfactory response . . . In every

instance, either through advice given or interaction, the onus was placed on me to deal with the issue."

Morrissey walked to a lonely coal tower near the campus on July 30, 2010 and fatally shot himself in the head. He left a suicide note. "I can't bear it anymore," wrote Morrissey.

While exonerating Genoways and the university in Morrissey's death, the university investigation concluded that Genoways had "questionable" managerial skills and called for revamping the university's complaint practices. Genoways remained in his post at VQR until 2012.

Employer's Responsibility

Suffice to say, both Braun and Morrissey felt bullied by their supervisors and both committed suicide. Morrissey reportedly suffered from depression and was worried that if he was fired he could not find another job because he did not have a college diploma. Some of Braun's co-workers called Braun a bully. Who is to blame? These are legal and philosophical questions. But it is possible – maybe even probable - that either or both deaths could have been averted if their employers had adequate processes in place to deal with workplace conflict, ranging from management training and oversight to appropriate complaint-handling techniques.

The U.S. Department of Justice's Bureau of Justice Statistics reports that workplace suicides in the United States rose to an all-time high in 2009, when there were 263 cases of workplace suicide. A preliminary count of workplace suicides showed a slight decline to 258 cases in 2010. Even with the decline, the 2010 preliminary count of workplace suicides is the third highest annual total for the fatal work injury census. (See: *See* http://www.bls.gov/news.release/cfoi.nr0.html , retrieved 12/23/11

In addition to health risks, targets of workplace bullying face severe financial consequences. If they are fired or forced to quit, they lose their income, health insurance, retirement benefits, etc. These losses can add up to larger problems, such as home foreclosure or automobile repossession. If the target cannot find a new job, he or she may have to seek taxpayer-funded public benefits. If the target does find a new job, it may be at a lower salary, or it may require relocation to different geographical area. Many employers today refuse to pay relocation costs to new hires. Older targets may never be able to find another job in their field due to rampant age discrimination in our society. Many targets of workplace bullying suffer severe financial losses for years and some for the rest of their lives.

Kathie Gant-- the woman who worked for the terrorizing attorney -- told the Maryland General Assembly that her bullying supervisor finally left for another job. But six months later a co-worker informed her that her former supervisor had returned to the office for a visit. Gant said she felt a resurgence of the panic she had experienced while working for the supervisor. "So I hid until she was gone," Gant said, through tears.

Gant said she never really recovered from the bullying. She said she was haunted by memories of her former boss calling her "stupid," humiliating her at meetings, and sending out office e-mails that belittled her work. She said the lawyer destroyed her reputation among other managers and co-workers. Gant finally quit her job and went back to school to study for a doctorate and to bolster her self-confidence. "[I]f I ever see her again, I'll be ready," said Gant.

Learning on the job

Frank, 22, a college student, was excited to begin his first real job at a hotel as a night desk clerk. Four months later, he was at the emergency room, thinking he was having a heart attack. It was diagnosed as work-related stress.

Frank (not his real name) said the night supervisor, a man in his 50s who had worked there for six years, routinely belittled and humiliated him -- for even minor mistakes. "I cannot make my own decisions here," the young worker said. "If even the slightest, most unimportant breach of rules takes place, I am met with threats that I will lose my job."

He complained to the owner of the hotel to no avail. The owner told Frank not to worry because "that's just how (he) is; he's really picky."

So Frank works silently and worries. "With a somewhat uncaring staff and a health problem, what should I do? I absolutely cannot lose this job; I'm trying to put myself through college."

3. ASSESS AND ANALYZE

"Normally, it takes years to work your way up to the twenty-seventh floor. But it only takes 30 seconds to be out on the street again. You dig?"
-J.D. Sheldrake to subordinate, C.C. Baxter in the 1960 movie, The Apartment

I was driving across country to start my new job at a domestic violence organization and had stopped at a fast food restaurant for a quick bite. I answered a call on my cell phone and a perky voice on the other end said, "Hi, I'm your new supervisor!"

There was a management shake-up. The supervisor who had interviewed and hired me would not be supervising me after-all. My new boss was a woman 25 years younger than me who had far less experience and no management background. She did not attend any of my interviews. We had never even met.

During my job interview, I made a point of saying that I didn't work well in a micro-managing environment. I was assured this was not an issue at the organization. I soon discovered, however, that my new supervisor's management style was akin to a Body Glove Super Stretch Wetsuit on an Olympic diver. She was highly critical and second guessed every move. Any question was treated as insubordination and evidence of lack of knowledge. She was an obsessive clock watcher. She yelled behind closed doors, withheld information needed for assignments, set unreasonable deadlines, and more.

Thus began my education in hardcore workplace bullying.

The Art of War is an ancient Chinese military treatise by Sun Tzu, a military general and strategist in the late sixth century, BC. He advised that a complete analysis is required before one enters into a confrontational situation. He emphasized the importance of positioning, after analyzing both objective and subjective conditions. To Sun Tzu, a plan should not be set in stone, but should be flexible -- allowing for a quick and appropriate response to an ever-changing situation. Good advice for targets of bullying as well as military officers.

Bullies engage in "take no prisoners" warfare. If a target does not show blind subservience, a bully will try to kill the target's spirit, ruin their reputation and drive them from the workplace. Bullies will lie, cheat, claim credit for the target's work and use sabotage to undermine the target. All the while, they show pleasant, even charming, face to their supervisors and to the Human Resources professionals who respond to your complaints.

Targets often are confused, embarrassed or in denial about what is happening to them. They may resist believing that a co-worker or supervisor is engaged in calculated, vicious, and unprovoked bullying. Many targets do not comprehend the bully's purpose until it's too late. By the time the employee understands that s/he is the target of a campaign of abuse, the bully may have had the time to set in place a cascading series of negative events – including written warnings and poor-job-performance reviews – that doom the target's future in the workplace.

As soon as a target realizes that workplace bullying is taking place, s/he should step back and assess the problem. What is the bully's motivation? Is the bully acting with the support of his or her superiors to achieve a strategic goal – such as downsizing without paying unemployment compensation? Is the bullying an outgrowth of a difficult working environment, such as staff role confusion, an increasing workload following a lay-off, an environment of intense competition, etc. Does the bully feel threatened by the target? Is the bully parroting the management style of other senior executives? Does the bully have a personality disorder? Analyzing the type of bullying that is taking place can shed light on what solutions, if any, are available.

I arrived at my former workplace during a time of great upheaval. The organization had been sued by a former employee who was fired after raising questions about the organization's handling of federal grants. The former employee then complained to federal authorities, resulting in an investigation. The case was settled when the organization agreed in 2008 to pay $300,000 to the U.S. Department of Justice to settle claims that it overcharged the federal government. The organization's director paid $16,500 of her own money to settle claims that her husband improperly received $94,000 in real estate commissions for helping the organization secure new office space. The fired employee received an undisclosed sum that was reportedly in excess of $100,000. And it all started with management's failure to address one employee's apparently valid complaint.

Criminal

Laura, a paralegal, heard a loud crash and then a shrieking sound. She ran into the senior partner's office and saw his secretary cowering in a corner. The partner overturned a file cabinet in anger because of a typing error in a pleading. A few weeks later, the partner threw a tape dispenser at the secretary, striking her leg, and the secretary quit. "She didn't even ask for any sort of severance package or compensation, which I attributed to her being freakin' terrified of the guy," said Laura (not her real name).

There is no law against workplace bullying, but there are laws against assault and battery. The criminal laws of a state apply equally in a back alley and a corporate boardroom. The secretary could have filed a criminal complaint against her boss, possibly to be followed-up with a civil lawsuit seeking monetary damages. The fact that her assailant was entrusted by his employer with supervisory authority does not exempt him from the obligation to abide by the criminal laws of the state.

Workplace bullying exists on the same spectrum of abuse as intimate partner or elder or child abuse –all of which carry potentially serious criminal sanctions. Yet, workplace bullying is rarely viewed with the same seriousness. What would happen, for example, if a teacher threw a tape dispenser at a student? It's not difficult to find reports of teachers who are prosecuted criminally for hitting students with physical objects. A teacher in Salt Lake City, Utah, was charged with one count of misdemeanor child abuse in 2011 for allegedly hitting a student with her violin bow after the student played his instrument out of turn during a music class.

Every state has a law that relates to bullying in educational institutions.

One of the first questions that targets and employers should consider in any bullying situation is whether any criminal laws are being or were broken. The potential scope of criminal behavior is endless, but here are some possible scenarios and questions:

- The bully physically intimidates, shoves the target, or otherwise causes the target to be physically injured – assault and/or battery?

- The bully won't let the target leave an enclosed space, such as an office or bathroom – false imprisonment?

- The bully stalks the target or makes harassing threats – criminal harassment?

– The bully invades the target's privacy. For example, a student who staged an internet broadcast of his roommate's homosexual encounter in his dorm room at Rutgers University in New Jersey in 2010 was convicted of invasion of privacy. (The roommate, Tyler Clementi, jumped to his death from New York's George Washington Bridge on September 22, 2010.)

Employers who ignore criminal behavior invite fines, penalties and lawsuits that carry potential liability for damages stemming from those acts.

Targets who ignore criminal behavior risk their health and safety and possible escalation of the violence.

Cyberbullying

One aspect of bullying in America has become a focus of criminal law– cyberbullying or electronic harassment.

Cyberbullying involves the use of the Internet and related technologies, such as mobile phones, to torment, harass, threaten, embarrass or otherwise harm another person. Often the bully hides behind anonymity while sending or posting harmful text or images to a wider audience. The National Crime Prevention Council asserts that cyberbullying can have the same debilitating effects as face-to-face bullying, including depression, loss of self-esteem, suicide and violence.

The Cyberbullying Research Institute reported in 2011 that ten states had adopted legislation calling for criminal sanctions for cyberbullying, including Arizona, Idaho, Kentucky, Louisiana, Missouri, Nevada, North Carolina, North Dakota, Tennessee and Wisconsin.

In Arizona, it is a felony to "anonymously or otherwise" contact, communicate or cause a communication with another person by verbal, electronic, mechanical, telegraphic, telephonic or written means in a manner that harasses. The term "harassment" refers to "conduct that is directed at a specific person and that would cause a reasonable person to be seriously alarmed, annoyed or harassed and the conduct in fact seriously alarms annoys or harasses the person." (Ariz. Rev. Stat. 13-2921 & 21.01).

The U.S. Congress held hearings in 2009 on a proposed criminal law to address cyber-bullying that was introduced by U.S. Rep. Linda T. Sanchez of California after the suicide of 13- year-old teenager. Megan Meier was bullied on a social networking site by Lori Drew, the mother of one of Meier's fellow students. Drew, 48, was convicted by a jury of three misdemeanor counts of violating the federal Computer Fraud and Abuse Act by using a fake Myspace account to harass Meier. A judge later overturned Drew's conviction, however, rejecting the government's novel theory that violating Myspace's terms of service was the legal equivalent of computer hacking.

Sanchez' proposed bill, called the Megan Meier Cyberbullying Prevention Act, was still pending in Congress in 2011. It states:

> "Whoever transmits in interstate or foreign commerce any communication, with the intent to coerce, intimidate, harass, or cause substantial emotional distress to a person, using electronic means to support severe, repeated, and hostile behavior, shall be fined under this title or imprisoned not more than two years, or both."

Cyberbullying is not just a problem in the school system. It is emerging as a problem in the workplace as well.

In August 2011, an employee for the state of Nevada, Sherry Truell, complained that her boss posted a "rant" about her on his personal Facebook page after she requested sick time under the Family and Medical Leave Act. Her son was facing surgery. Among other things, Truell's boss, Steven Zuelke, wrote: "Why is it that for some people FMLA stands for Family Medical Leave Act and for others, it should stand for Fire My Lazy Ass?" Fortunately for Truell, she was represented by a union, which filed a grievance on her behalf. The grievance resulted in Zuelke's suspension, even though Nevada had no policy at the time governing an employee's use of social media.

Most foreign jurisdictions have addressed the general problem of workplace bullying as either a health and safety issue or a civil matter. The Parliament in Victoria, Australia, however, voted in June, 2011, to bring serious workplace bullying within the Commonwealth's criminal definition of stalking. Serious bullying includes "threats and abusive words or acts" and now carries a possible ten year prison sentence.

Victoria's law is named "Brodie's Law" after Brodie Panlock, a 19-year-old cafe worker who killed herself in 2006 after being relentlessly bullied by four colleagues. A coroner's inquest determined that she committed suicide because of the bullying. Brodie's tormenters entered guilty pleas and were fined $432,337 under Australia's occupational safety and health act. But Brodie's father, Damian Panlock, considered the fines to be a "slap on the wrist." He campaigned successfully for the adoption of criminal sanctions.

Various other criminal laws in the United States address specific types of bullying and may be applicable to the workplace. These laws include criminal harassment, stalking, assault and battery, false imprisonment, sexual assault, and homicide. The vast majority of workplace bullying, however, does not involve the type of threats and physical violence that tend to result in criminal prosecution. Workplace bullying is usually accomplished through myriad small acts that of and by themselves do not fit within the definition of a criminal statute – but which add up to serious health endangering violence.

Even if a particular case of workplace bullying does not give rise to criminal prosecution, it can provoke criminal violence in the workplace. The term "going postal" was inspired by a series of lethal shootings of postal workers by disgruntled employees of the U.S. Postal Service in the 1980s. If a company fails to address and prevent incivility in the workplace, it can escalate to aggressive forms of workplace violence. (*See* Andersson, L. M., & Pearson, C. M., Tit *for tat? The spiraling effect of incivility in the Workplace*, Academy of Management Review, *24*, 452-471 (1999))

In 2010, a nine-year Walmart employee, John Gillane, 46, said he shot three of his supervisors in Reno, NV, because he felt he was not being fairly treated. Among other things, he complained that one of the supervisors who did not know him well gave him a poor evaluation. Gillane, who had a history of mental illness, told police that he wanted to "get even" and make Walmart pay. "Was I disgruntled? – yeah, I was disgruntled. I was going to take on Goliath," he said.

Civil law

Workplace bullying obviously is taken quite seriously in Victoria, Australia. This is reflected by the fact that severe bullying violates criminal law. In the United States, workplace bullying generally is viewed less seriously. It is treated as a civil matter. Each of the 21 American states that have considered proposed legislation to address workplace bullying has considered legislation that would create a civil cause of action. As of 2011, no state had actually approved workplace anti-bully legislation.

In a criminal case, society is considered to be a victim of the harm (which is defined by the federal or state the legislature as a criminal act). A prosecutor or grand jury acts on behalf of society to prosecute the alleged offender. If convicted, the offender can suffer one of the harshest sanctions available to society, loss of freedom. The standard of proof in a criminal case is guilt beyond a reasonable doubt, reflecting the possibility that the defendant could lose his or her freedom and be jailed.

In a civil matter, an individual – the plaintiff – asks the court to order the defendant to pay compensation for damages resulting from the defendant's actions or failure to act. The plaintiff's standard of proof is only that it is more probable than not that the damage occurred. Proposed workplace bully legislation adopts a "reasonable person" standard; it means that the alleged behavior is judged from the perspective of a reasonable person exercising ordinary care, skill and judgment.

Whether or not it is appropriate to treat workplace bullying as a civil matter, it definitely has ramifications for the target. It is up to the individual target, and not society, to "prosecute" the offender. This can be a particularly onerous task for an individual who has suffered months or years of bullying. Many targets lack the mental and physical stamina to find an attorney, file a lawsuit and participate in a lengthy adversarial process. And many targets ultimately are fired or quit and also lack the financial resources to wage a lengthy court battle against a well-funded employer.

It is increasingly difficult for most Americans – not just targets – to pursue their rights in the U.S. civil justice system. The World Justice Institute's 2011 study of legal systems across the globe shows the United States ranks far behind other countries on providing an accessible legal system to the public. The U.S. ranked 21st out of the 66 countries in assuring access to the legal system. The United States' lowest score was in "Access to Legal Counsel" and "Access and Affordability of Civil Courts." With respect to affordability of legal counsel, the U.S. ranked 52nd out of the 66 countries studied. "Legal assistance is expensive or unavailable, and the gap between rich and poor individuals in terms of both actual use of and satisfaction with the civil courts system remains significant," states the report's authors.

The bottom line is that American workers have a more difficult time than workers in many other countries accessing the civil justice system to enforce their rights and to prevent employers from engaging in workplace bullying. The United States policy of shifting responsibility for the problem of workplace bullying to individual targets also does nothing to address the systemic problem of strategic harassment by employers.

Duty to Provide a Safe Workplace

All American employers are required to provide a safe workplace for employees by the General Duty Clause of the Occupational Safety and Health Act of 1970.

The Occupational Safety and Health Administration, which administers the OSH Act, has ignored workplace bullying as a national problem, despite overwhelming research showing that workplace bullying can cause severe damage to a target's mental and physical health. But OSHA in 2011 adopted a workplace bullying policy that covers its own employees.

OSHA's anti-bully policy requires all OSHA employees to "treat all other employees, as well as customers, with dignity and respect. Management will provide a working environment as safe as possible by having preventative measures in place and by dealing immediately with threatening or potentially violent situations. No employee will engage in threats, violent outbursts, intimidations, *bullying harassment*, or other abusive or disruptive behaviors." (Italics added)

If a workplace bully policy is necessary to insure a safe working environment for OSHA employees, one wonders why OSHA has not acted to insure that all American receive the same or equivalent protections?

Definitions of Workplace Bullying

As previously noted, there is no current uniformly-accepted legal definition of workplace bullying in the United States. What follows is a general overview of how workplace bullying is defined from several different perspectives. These definitions have common elements, including recognition that workplace bullying usually involves negative or hostile behaviors that occur repeatedly over time with the intent of harming the target and/or the target's work. In some cases, a single instance of bullying would be sufficient to be actionable if it was particularly egregious. Most of the time, it is understood that a power imbalance exists between the parties, and that the targets feel unable to defend themselves.

International Definition

The United States is behind the curve in addressing workplace bullying, which has been studied for more than two decades in Europe. In many other industrialized countries, workplace bullying is considered a violation of a worker's inherent right to dignity and the source of potentially serious health and safety problems that could negatively impact the economy. International scholars and experts from countries that have adopted workplace bully laws and regulations agree upon the following general definition of workplace bullying:

> – Harassing, offending, socially excluding someone or negatively affecting someone's work tasks.

– The interaction or process occurs repeatedly and regularly (e.g. weekly) and over a period of time (e.g. about six months).

– The process escalates until the person confronted ends up in an inferior position and becomes the target of systematic negative social acts.

* From Katherine Lippel, *Introduction*, 32 Comp. Labor Law & Pol'y Journal 2 (2010), *citing* Stale Einarsen et al., *The Concept of Bullying and Harassment at Work: The European Tradition*, in Stale Einarsen, et al, Bullying and Harassment in the Workplace: Development in Theory, Research and Practice, 3, 32 (2d ed., 2011).

World Health Organization

The World Health Organization (WHO) says that workplace mobbing or bullying is a form of employee abuse that seriously negatively impacts an individual's health and quality of life, mainly in the emotional, psychosomatic and behavioral areas. According to the WHO, the following are examples of workplace bullying:

–Exclusion.

–Slander, gossiping, rumors.

–Humiliation.

–Turning co-workers against the victim.

-Intrusions into private life.

-Isolation.

-Provocation.

-Ridicule, especially in the presence of others.

-Taking away key areas of the target's responsibilities.

-Threats of violence.

-Verbal abuse.

-Assignment of meaningless tasks.

-Assignment of new duties without training.

-Excessive monitoring of the person.

-Forced inactivity.

-Intentionally underrating or ignoring proposals.

-Remote unjustified transfers.

-Repeated criticism and blame.

-Withholding information essential for target's performance.

-Unjustifiably low merit rating.

-Unjustified disciplinary action.

-Work overload with impossible deadlines.

International Labour Organization

The International Labour Organization (ILO) considers workplace bullying and physical violence at work to be on the same level of seriousness. "The new profile of violence at work ... gives equal emphasis to physical and psychological behaviour, and one which gives full recognition to the significance of minor acts of violence," says Vittorio Di Martino, co-author of a 2009 ILO report on workplace bullying.

The ILO defines workplace bullying as offensive behavior, including vindictive, cruel, malicious or humiliating attempts to undermine an individual or groups of employees by, among other things:

- Making life difficult for those who have the potential to do the bully's job better.

- Shouting at staff to get things done.

- Insisting that the "bully's way is the right way."

- Refusing to delegate, because the bully feels no one else can be trusted.

- Punishing others by constant criticism.

- Removing the target's responsibilities because he or she is too competent and may outshine the bully.

* From: International Labour Organization, *When Working Becomes Hazardous*, 26 World of Work 6 (1998).

Efforts in to pass an anti-bully law in the US

California was the first state to consider workplace anti-bullying legislation in the United States in 2003. The proposed bill, which did not pass, was called the "Healthy Workplace Bill" (HWB). It was drafted by David C. Yamada, a professor of law at Suffolk University.

Gary and Ruth Namie, founders of the Workplace Bullying Institute made Yamada's proposed bill the focal point of the Institute's state-by-state campaign to pass workplace bullying legislation. By 2013, twenty four states had considered some version of the HWB but no state had adopted it.

The original HWB was very restrictive and would limit redress to all but the most onerous cases of workplace bullying. The law was revised in 2013 but still lacks protections afforded to workers in other countries.

In the HWB, Yamada defined abusive conduct as:

> "...conduct, including acts, omissions, or both, that a reasonable person would find hostile, based on the severity, nature, and frequency of the defendant's conduct."

Specifically, the HWB stated that "abusive conduct" may include but is not limited to:

> – Repeated infliction of verbal abuse such as the use of derogatory remarks, insults, and epithets;

- Verbal or physical conduct of a threatening, intimidating, or humiliating nature;

- The sabotage or undermining of an employee's work performance;

- Attempts to exploit an employee's known psychological or physical vulnerability.

A single act normally will not constitute abusive conduct, but an especially severe and egregious act may meet this standard.

Some experts favor a bill proposed by a Nevada legislature over the HWB.

State Senator Richard "Tick" Segerblom of Las Vegas in 2009 and 2011 proposed amending the definition of a "hostile work environment" in the Nevada civil rights law that parallels Title VII in the Civil Rights Act of 1964. Segerblom proposed expanding the umbrella of employees who are protected from working in a hostile workplace under Title VII to all employees. Presently, the Title VII only protects workers who are subjected to a hostile work environment because of discrimination on the basis of race, color, religion, sex (including pregnancy), national origin, age (40 or older), disability or genetic information. Essentially, Segerblom proposed a "status blind" definition of Title VII with respect to hostile work environment claims.

Segerblom's bill defines "abusive conduct" as:

– Repeated verbal abuse in the form of derogatory remarks, insults and epithets.

– Verbal or physical conduct which is threatening, intimidating and humiliating, and;

– The gratuitous sabotage or undermining of a person's work product.

– The behavior must be severe or pervasive enough to create a workplace environment that a reasonable person would consider intimidating, hostile, or abusive.

In both the proposed Healthy Workplace Bill and Sen. Segerblom's bill, an employer could escape liability for a hostile work environment by exercising reasonable care to prevent the abusive conduct, and by promptly correcting the abusive conduct.

Equal Employment Opportunity Commission

The U.S. Equal Employment Commission, which is charged with enforcing federal employment discrimination laws, says harassment is:

"Unwelcome conduct that is based on race, color, religion, sex (including pregnancy), national origin, age (40 or older), disability or genetic information."

Harassment becomes unlawful, according to the EEOC, when the target is subjected to a hostile workplace environment. This occurs where "enduring the offensive conduct becomes a condition of continued employment, or the conduct is severe or pervasive enough to create a work environment that a reasonable person would consider intimidating, hostile, or abusive."

School Anti-Bully Laws

Almost every state has passed anti-bullying legislation that is designed to thwart student-to-student bullying in educational institutions. Targets of workplace bullying can look to the anti-bullying statute in their state to see how their legislature defines school bullying. One could argue that this definition also should apply to the workplace.

Massachusetts, for example, passed a tough school anti-bullying law in 2010 that contains the following definition:

> Bullying is the repeated use by one or more students of a written, verbal or electronic expression or a physical act or gesture or any combination thereof, directed at a victim that: causes physical or emotional harm to the victim or damage to the victim's property; places the victim in reasonable fear of harm to himself or of damage to his property; creates a hostile environment at school for the victim; Infringes on the rights of the victim at school; or materially and substantially disrupts the education process or the orderly operation of a school.

The bill defines a "hostile environment" as "a situation in which bullying causes the school environment to be permeated with intimidation, ridicule or insult that is sufficiently severe or pervasive to alter the conditions of the student's education."

4. BEING BULLIED?

"Find out what people will submit to, and you have found out the exact amount of injustice which will be imposed upon them."

- Frederick Douglass

Fear and Loathing in the American Workplace

One morning you sit down at your desk and you realize that something is wrong. Maybe the director walked by without saying "hello," or your co-workers failed to invite you to join them for lunch. But it's more than that. You feel uncomfortable and oddly vulnerable. It is as if you have a twinge in your side that portends trouble.

Unrelated incidents come to mind. You didn't receive notice of a committee meeting that you normally are invited to attend. Come to think of it, your supervisor hasn't spoken to you for several days. You feel the stirrings of panic in your stomach. "Could I be in trouble?" You feel dread as you imagine the turmoil of being without a paycheck for both you and your family.

Targets of workplace bullying live with emotional chaos. Bullying supervisors may alternate between intense micromanagement, and periods of inexplicable neglect. Bullies

56

work behind the scenes to discredit the target. They convince other managers that the target is incompetent. Co-workers stay away, sensing trouble.

In the midst of a busy office, a target feels a profound sense of loneliness.

Workplace bullying is a well-known problem in Europe but it is only now beginning to be understood in the United States. It is still roughly in the place as domestic violence in the 1970s, when society began to stop telling abused women to go home and try to be better wives. A rash of highly-publicized teen suicides in recent years has raised awareness of school bullying. Some of the awareness of the negative consequences of school bullying has spilled over into the workplace. Academics, social scientists and other types of experts realize that workplace bullying is an important human rights and public health issue. But, as yet, nothing much is being done about it.

A complicating factor with respect to workplace bullying is the existence of inherent inequality in the employer/employee relationship. The employer exercises authority and control over workers. Supervisors evaluate the performance of the employee, and not vice-versa. The employer signs the employee's paycheck. And there can be a fine line between appropriate but exacting supervision and inappropriate bullying.

It is important to recognize that legitimate and reasonable management techniques may have adverse consequences for some workers. This is not the same thing as bullying. Reasonable management techniques may include:

- Providing appropriate feedback on work performance.
- Managing performance or underperformance issues.
- Issuing reasonable directions about work allocation.
- Enforcement of attendance policy.
- Transferring a staff member or layoffs (where the process is conducted fairly and equitably).
- Making justifiable decisions related to recruitment, selection and other development opportunities.
- Implementing workplace policies.
- Managing allegations of misconduct and using disciplinary actions where appropriate.

Obviously, no workplace is perfect. Few employees have only good things to say about their supervisor. And more than one supervisor has observed, "To make an omelet, you may have to break a few eggs." A perfectly normal boss/worker relationship is sometimes bumpy and marked by tension. Some workers may be disgruntled – even in a bully-free workplace. But there is an important difference between normal conflict and abuse. When an employee complains of abuse, it is the responsibility of the employer to take the complaint seriously and to conduct an immediate investigation.

Employers control every aspect of the workplace. Employers alone have the power to stop workplace abuse. To paraphrase Franklin Delano Roosevelt said, "With great power comes great responsibility."

Baggage of Labor History

Even in the best of times, many workers have low expectations with respect to their jobs. They often do not recognize bullying at the outset.

Most people realize that their job will not always be pleasant and enjoyable. There will be unfairness, bureaucratic regulations, buzzing fluorescent lights, irritating co-workers and less than optimal pay. Someone else inevitably controls the air conditioning or heating unit. With some exceptions, most workers know that most jobs, at least some of the time, will be dispiriting, and unfulfilling.

These low expectations are not a fluke. There is a legacy of longstanding friction between management and labor that dates back to our nation's founding.

Indentured servants followed the Pilgrims off the boat when it docked in Plymouth, Massachusetts, in the early 1600s. Indentured servants were typically young people under the age of 21 who accepted passage to America in exchange for a term – often seven years – of unpaid labor. These servants endured long hours, violence, and even death. The employer owned the indentured servants "labor" during the period of servitude, but the servant could look forward to freedom once the debt was paid.

And that servitude – at least theoretically –was voluntary. African slaves, in contrast, were brought to America involuntarily, and most were treated as chattel – moveable property – until their death. They had little or no hope of release. That prospect endured until 1865, when Congress passed the Thirteenth Amendment to the United States Constitution.

American history is replete with instances of company union bashing, violent strikes and general labor unrest and the friction continues today. In May 2011, Wisconsin Gov. Scott Walker signed a bill taking away nearly all collective bargaining rights from the vast majority of the state's public employees. This action followed a three-week battle that saw all Democratic state senators flee to neighboring Illinois and as many as 80,000 citizens protest at the Capitol building.

The bottom line is that many American workers are pre-programmed to put up with a certain amount of on-the-job misery. Targets of bullying may be initially puzzled by their supervisor's negative behavior, thinking s/he is having a bad day or is simply an "odd duck." Or perhaps the target feels that s/he is being overly sensitive. Targets may instinctively know on some level that something is going on that does not bode well – but what?

Employees who are bullied often soldier on in the hope that things will get better – losing valuable time to respond to the problem. By the time workplace becomes a truly painful place, it is clear that the target is under assault. Targets may spend much of their time worrying about and re-thinking their problems in the workplace. On Monday morning, they wake up with a feeling of dread. At work, they are on edge. Scared even. What new injury will today bring? Humiliation. The silent treatment. Isolation. Unfair criticism. A dreaded pink slip?

Considering the high prevalence of workplace bullying, and the usual outcome (most targets are fired or quit), it is definitely to an employee's advantage to be knowledgeable about and alert to the problem of workplace bullying. At the first signs of bullying, a target should be thinking about how to respond. It may be too late after the bullying supervisor has cited the employee for bogus infractions or compiled negative employment-evaluations.

Research shows that workers who are bullied suffer a wide range of mental and physical damage, including:

- Distress, anxiety and panic attacks.

- Impaired concentration or ability to make decisions.

- Loss of self-esteem and confidence, a sense of isolation or withdrawal from the workplace.

- Physical illness, including digestive problems, skin conditions, headaches and musculoskeletal disorders.

- Sleep disturbance.

- Reduced quality of home and family life.

- Substance or drug abuse.

– In extreme cases, risk of suicide or violence.

Some targets may even develop brief psychotic episodes, generally with paranoid symptoms.

The damage incurred by a target is often in proportion to the intensity and duration of bullying. Researchers have identified distinct phases of bullying, each leading to enhanced stress:

– Conflict, often characterized by a 'critical incident.'

– Aggressive acts; bullying and stigmatizing.

– Management involvement.

– Branding as difficult or mentally ill.

– Expulsion or resignation from the workplace.

Source: N. Davenport, R.D. Schwartz, G.P. Elliott. *Mobbing: Emotional Abuse in the American Workplace 38.* *(*1999).

At some point, most targets experience constant and debilitating stress. And not just at the workplace. All the time.

———————

The Bully's Toolkit

Here are some tactics that are widely recognized as signs of bullying:

- Glaring.

- Flaunting status.

- Ignoring the worker or his/her contributions.

- Interrupting and preventing expression.

- Failing to respond to calls or memos.

- The silent treatment.

- Verbal attacks.

- Shouting.

- Spreading gossip.

- Blaming the target for mistakes made by others.

- Swearing at the worker.

- Excluding the worker from important activities and meetings.

- Making obscene or offensive gestures.

- Playing mean pranks.

– Moving target's desk or office to remote area to humiliate target.

———————

Bullying Behaviors

Workers who suspect they are being bullied probably are being bullied. A scientific 2011 CareerBuilder survey of 5,671 U.S. workers found that more than one in four (27 percent) felt bullied in the workplace. And the bully was most often a supervisor. According to the CareerBuilder survey, targets reported these common complaints:

– My comments were dismissed or not acknowledged – 43 percent.

– I was falsely accused of mistakes I didn't make – 40 percent.

– I was harshly criticized – 38 percent.

– I was forced into doing work that really wasn't my job – 38 percent.

– Different standards and policies were used for me than other workers – 37 percent.

– I was given mean looks – 31 percent.

– Others gossiped about me – 27 percent.

- My boss yelled at me in front of other co-workers – 24 percent.

- Belittling comments were made about my work during meetings – 23 percent.

- Someone else stole credit for my work – 21 percent.

The first book to introduce the concept of workplace bullying to a United States audience was published in 1999, *Mobbing: Emotional Abuse in the American Workplace,* by Noa Zanolli Davenport, Ruth D. Schwartz, and Gail P. Elliott. The co-authors wrote that the harm suffered by targets of workplace bullying is analogous to the first, second and third degree burns suffered by fire victims:

- First degree: Victim manages to resist, escapes at an early stage, or is fully rehabilitated in the original workplace or elsewhere;

- Second degree: Victim cannot resist or escape immediately and suffers temporary or prolonged mental and/or physical disability and has difficulty reentering the workforce;

- Third degree: Victim is unable to re-enter the workforce and suffers serious, long-lasting mental or physical disability.

Few targets of bullying emerge from the nightmare unscathed. It is a traumatic experience for almost every target and, for many, it affects every aspect of their lives.

A Target's Narrative

"I worked for a female boss who was going through some sort of drug therapy to help her conceive a baby. The extra hormones, tests and anti-depressants that she was prescribed made her very difficult to work with. She belittled me in front of others and was extremely sarcastic and passive aggressive toward me. What made it worse was that upper management defended her behavior because she was going through a 'tough time.'

I finally left the company after I was accused of being negative toward her. I was demoralized and very angry.

Upon reflection, it was a very traumatic and stressful time. I was consumed with an obsession to talk about it. If I saw her now, I would walk right past her in the street because I would find it too emotional to talk to her.

At the end of the day people leave jobs because of other people. Companies need to prevent power-hungry bosses and co-workers from inflicting their personal issues upon their staff."

Why Me?

There are many theories about why an individual is targeted by a bully. Some research shows the reason has more to do with the bully than the target. For example, highly competent and popular employees may be targeted because they are considered to be a threat to the bully. Organizational cultures and leadership styles may foster bullying behaviors – which is why bullying is thought to be more prevalent in certain workplaces (i.e. government administration, hospitals, schools, and prisons). And a company may engage intentionally in strategic harassment to achieve an organizational goal, such as to boost short-term productivity. Sometimes a target just has the bad luck to work for a boss who is a psychopath, lacking in empathy.

A 2011 article in *The International Journal of Business and Social Science* suggests that there are three reasons that individuals become targets of workplace bullying:

> – Differences in age, race, gender, ethnicity, and educational levels may intensify conflicts and increase bullying behaviors because people do not understand the motivations and actions of people who are perceived as different.

> – Individuals who lack self-confidence or sufficient conflict management skills are more likely to be targets of workplace bullying,

> – People who are characterized as overachievers may fall prey to a workplace bully because the bully feels threatened by the target's competence. Bullying may

result from a manager's need to boost his or herself worth and undermine a subordinate as a result of feeling envious of a subordinate's talents or work ethic.

* Source: A. Georgakopoulos et al, *Workplace Bullying: A Complex Problem in Contemporary Organizations,* 2 International Journal of Business and Social Science 3 (Special Issue – January 2011).

Research also indicates that older women are most vulnerable to being bullied.

The 2011 CareerBuilder survey found that one-third (34 percent) of women said they have felt bullied in the workplace compared to 22 percent of men. The CareerBuilder survey found that two age groups were most likely to report feeling bullied – workers ages 55 or older (29 percent), and workers age 24 or younger (29 percent). Hence, older women report feeling most bullied. A similar conclusion was reached in a scientific 2010 poll by Zogby International. The Zogby survey found that 58 percent of targets of bullying are women, while 42 percent are men.

Conversely, the Zogby survey found that most bullies – an estimated 62 percent -- are males. Interestingly, male bullies don't seem to discriminate on the basis of gender; their victims are about 50-50 male and female. Whereas, the survey found that women bullies victimize woman over men about 80 percent of the time.

A study by psychologists at the University of Cincinnati lends credence to the stereotype of the Queen Bee– the bossy woman in the office who bullies other workers, usually women. The researchers found that women tend to be "cogs in the machine" to other women in the workplace. Also, a female boss is more likely to wreck a woman's promotion prospects in male-dominated environments. Men who report to a female manager tend to get more mentoring and support than their female colleagues. The psychologists speculate that women who manage to break the glass ceiling and become managers may not want competition from other women and/or may want to blend in as much as possible with their male counterparts. *(See* David J. Maume, *Meet the new boss...same as the old boss? Female supervisors and subordinate career prospects,* Social Science Research, Volume 40, Issue 1, January 2011.)

The real importance of the Cincinnati study, however, may be that it demonstrates that workplaces remain male-oriented in their customs, policies, and structures. And female bosses, like male bosses, tend to follow traditional organizational preferences to invest in men's careers more so than women's.

In the final analysis, the real issue is not so much why a target is chosen by a bully for abuse as it is whether the employer tolerated the abusive behavior. Once a target complains to an employer that s/he is being abused, the employer has a legal obligation to act immediately to stop the abuse. Failure to act can expose the employer to significantly greater liability in a lawsuit.

Bullying the Boss

Most bullies are bosses or managers but that does not mean that bosses and managers are immune from bullying.

Ron (not his real name) served as the chief executive officer for several different organizations in a distinguished career. He still recalls a particular member of the board of directors of one organization who was a bully. Even at his job interview, he noticed the board member was frowning in a disapproving way. "This guy was like a cat waiting to pounce. He looked for opportunities to question my judgment, my performance, and my ability to lead. Nothing I could do was good enough. He eventually poisoned the board against me. I had to leave."

In another case, a manager faced resistance from former team members after she was promoted over her former supervisor during a company restructuring. The former supervisor was very popular and well liked, and employees resented the new manager's promotion. They were disobedient and rude. The new manager finally turned to senior management for help. Not only did they not help her, but they left her with the impression that she was at fault. Isolated and helpless, she finally quit.

Employers too!

In this age of social media, even employers can be bullied. One disgruntled employee who shares his gripes on social media can potentially inflict grievous damage a firm's reputation. As Benjamin Franklin said: "It takes many good deeds to build a good reputation and only one bad one to lose it."

The Ethics Resource Center (ERC), a non-profit center based in Arlington, VA, that works to advance high ethical standards in public and private institutions, reported in 2011 that corporate executives who were surveyed estimated that 63 percent of their companies' market value is due to reputation. The ERC says a good reputation may be even more important for consumer product firms, where consumers cast verdicts on reputation with their pocketbooks, withholding business from companies they believe are ethically deficient, and rewarding those with good reputation.

An Ohio employer recognized the value of its good reputation when it was threatened. Kaufmann Racing Equipment, which specializes in building and selling racing auto parts, became the target of negative comments posted on several web sites popular with racing enthusiasts. At issue was a 2006 business deal that soured. Scott Roberts, a Virginia resident, purchased a Pontiac automobile motor from Kauffman. After having the motor for eight months, Roberts sent it back to the Kaufmann, claiming it was defective. Kaufmann refused to refund Roberts' money after learning that Roberts had modified the motor.

After Roberts began posting negative comments on the Internet, Kauffman filed a defamation lawsuit alleging that Roberts had waged a smear campaign against the company, accusing Kaufmann of selling defective engine blocks. Roberts had the case dismissed on grounds that the Ohio court lacked jurisdiction because Roberts lived out-of-state. An Ohio appeals court reinstated the case and Roberts appealed to the Ohio Supreme Court.

Ohio's high court, in a 4-2 decision, ruled the state's "long arm statute" permitted Roberts to be sued in Ohio because Roberts' comments could be accessed in Ohio and were clearly intended to hurt an Ohio business. (*Kauffman Racing Equip., L.L.C. v. Roberts*, No. 2008-1038 (Ohio 2010)

It was a bittersweet victory for Kaufmann, which had subsidized four years of litigation to be able to sue Roberts for damages in Ohio only. "We had to absolutely take this position because if we allow one person to do this, then everyone could do it and the line had to be drawn in the sand to let people know that businesses and people are not to be trifled with through use of the Internet," said Kaufmann's attorney, Brett Jaffee.

The vulnerability of a company's reputation in the Internet age has given rise to a new industry dedicated to protecting the online reputation of companies and professionals. One such company advertises: "A positive reputation can take 20 years to build and only five minutes to destroy. Maintaining a positive reputation online is critical to your success."

Perhaps the classic case of "what goes around comes around" in the context of workplace bullying involves Indiana University (IU) and its former basketball coach, Bobby Knight.

From 1971-2000, Knight led the Hoosiers to three NCAA titles. During that time, Knight threw a chair across the court during a game, nearly hitting people in the wheelchair section. He was charged with berating referees, choking a player, shoving a fan into a garbage can, chewing out IU cheerleaders, intimidating an IU executive and administrative staff, and routinely displaying a combative nature during encounters with members of the press.

Myles N. Brand, Ph.D., inherited Knight when he became IU's president in 1994. Brand placed Knight on a "zero tolerance" warning for termination in 1999 after Knight fired IU assistant basketball coach Ron Felling. When Knight overheard a phone call in which Felling criticized Knight's coaching and behavior, Knight allegedly threw Felling out of a chair. Despite the "zero tolerance" warning, Knight, in September 2000, allegedly grabbed the arm of an IU freshman and cursed at him after the student – in Knight's estimation -- failed to be properly deferential. The student reportedly said, "Hey, Knight, what's up?" Brand fired Knight.

Knight and his fans filed lawsuits and appeals against the university. Brand and IU athletic administrators became the focal point of bitter rancor and IU's athletic program suffered devastating instability that persisted for years. A former IU soccer coach, Jerry Yeagley, was quoted in 2011 as stating: "It tore apart the department and the university. Basically there was no middle ground; you were on one side or the other."

Two year after Knight left IU, he settled a lawsuit that Felling filed against him over the original incident. Knight agreed to pay Felling $25,000 and admitted that he had shoved Felling in anger. IU settled a lawsuit filed by Knight against IU that accused the University of failing to adequately represent Knight in the Felling lawsuit. Under the terms of the settlement, an IU alumni group agreed to pay Knight $75,000. Knight was awarded more in damages than Felling.

Knight went on to coach at Texas Tech University, where other instances of alleged bullying occurred. He was forcibly restrained by police after he was heckled by a Baylor University fan in 2006 and, the same year, appeared to hit Texas Tech player Michael Prince under the chin. Prince, his parents, and Texas Tech Athletic Director Gerald Myers insisted that Knight did nothing wrong and that he merely lifted Prince's chin and told him, "Hold your head up and don't worry about mistakes. Just play the game."

The IU/Knight saga should serve as a lesson for employers who tolerate bullies. In the long run, it can be an expensive and painful proposition.

5. ABOUT BULLIES

"All power tends to corrupt, and absolute power corrupts absolutely." - Lord Acton (1887).

Wired Differently

There are many complex reasons for workplace bullying. The employer may encourage managers to bully subordinates to achieve a short term goal. Or the employer may be complacent and fail to act in response to a hostile workplace environment. But often the reason is fairly straightforward. One individual seems to have a compulsion to bully others.

Workplace bullies may be "wired" differently. A magnetic resonance imaging study conducted by researchers at the University of Chicago in 2008 found that some bullies get pleasure out of seeing someone else's pain. The study involved brain scans of teens with a history of aggressive bullying behavior. Their empathetic response seemed to be distorted by activity in regions of the brain associated with reward and pleasure.

"We think it means that they like seeing people in pain," said Psychologist Benjamin Lahey, who worked on the study. "If that is true, they are getting positively reinforced every time they bully and are aggressive to other people." (See J. Decety, et al.,

Atypical empathic responses in adolescents with aggressive conduct disorder: A functional MRI investigation, 80 Biological Psychology, Issue 2, pp. 203-211 (2009))

Australian Forensic Psychologist John Clarke says there is a common misconception that psychopaths are violent criminals. He says there are more psychopaths in office buildings than in prisons. "The majority of them are living and working around us in jobs, psychologically destroying the people that they work with," said Clarke.

Clarke says workplace psychopaths are superficially charming, but ruthless, unremorseful, manipulative, intimidating, cold-blooded, calculating, and self-absorbed and totally lacking in empathy. There is "very little difference between compiling a psychological profile of a serial rapist and developing a profile of an organisational psychopath," writes Clarke. "Once the primary motivating factor of power and self-gratification is understood, it is simply a matter of following the path of destruction left by both types of psychopath." (See, John Clarke, *Working with Monsters: How to Identify and Protect Yourself from the Workplace Psychopath* (2005).

A former British academic advanced a theory that "corporate psychopaths" at the helm of financial institutions in the United States are largely to blame for the global financial meltdown. "They are happy to walk away from the economic disaster that they have managed to bring about, with huge payoffs and with new roles advising governments how to prevent such economic disasters," writes Clive R. Boddy, in his book, *Corporate Psychopaths: Organizational Destroyers* (2011). "Many of these people display several of the characteristics of psychopaths, and some of them are undoubtedly true psychopaths."

Boddy says psychopaths are the one percent of "people who, perhaps due to physical factors to do with abnormal brain connectivity and chemistry" lack a "conscience, have few emotions and display an inability to have any feelings, sympathy or empathy for other people." These people, Boddy adds, are "extraordinarily cold, much more calculating and ruthless towards others than most people are and therefore a menace to the companies they work for and to society."

Psychopaths make it to the top of successful corporations, Boddy says, because they take advantage of the "relative chaotic nature of the modern corporation," including "rapid change, constant renewal" and high turnover of "key personnel." They exhibit a combination of "charm" and "charisma," which makes "their behaviour invisible" and "makes them appear normal and even to be ideal leaders."

Boddy says that psychopaths destroy the morale and emotional well-being of fellow workers "by humiliating them, lying about them, abusing them, using organisational rules to control them, not giving them adequate training, blaming them for mistakes made by the psychopath, bullying them and coercing them into unwanted sexual activities

Psychological research lends support to the maxim that power corrupts. Individuals with power tend to pursue personal goals without concern for the social consequences of their actions. This leads to objectification, which is the process of viewing other people in terms of the qualities that make them useful to the perceiver as opposed to the qualities that allow them to be perceived as unique human beings. (*See* Joe C. Magee, et al., *Leadership and the psychology of power*, in D. M. Messick & R. Kramer (eds.), *The Psychology of Leadership: New Perspectives and Research* (2004).

In one study, participants were asked to draw an "E" on their foreheads. Subjects who identified themselves as powerful were three times as likely to draw the "E" so that it was illegible to observers (i.e. backward) but legible to themselves. People who felt less powerful drew the "E" so others could read it – it was illegible from their own perspective.

The researchers concluded that power may reduce one's ability to see the world through others' eyes, an effect that could lead to social exploitation. They suggested implementing "moderating factors" to reduce power differences, such as holding managers personally accountable for their actions and insuring that they are subject to having their power revoked if it is abused. (*See* Adam D. Galinsky, et al., *Power and Perspectives Not Taken,* 17 Psychological Science 12, 1068 (2006))

Another theory is more pessimistic. Bill Eddy, a social worker and attorney who co-founded the High Conflict Institute,

Scottsdale, AZ, says bullies at work are High Conflict People. They are not reacting to an external stimuli but, rather, bring this behavior with them to the job. He compares bullying to alcoholism. Eddy says the bully is in denial and resists change. He says it is futile for a target to confront a bully and that a simple reprimand by the employer is unlikely to change a bully's behavior.

Tough Boss?

Some conflict is normal in life. It is not realistic to think there will be no conflict in the workplace. It is the job of a supervisor to enforce the policies and rules in the workplace and this may naturally leads to employee resistance or complaints. However, appropriate supervision of employees is not the equivalent of bullying. An employer can discipline or fire an employee with due process, respect and dignity. In other words, it is possible to identify a substandard employee and take action without abusing the employee.

A tough boss might not like your work and may even fire you, but that doesn't make him or her a bully. A bully is motivated by a personal need or desire to dominate and control the target by whatever means are necessary. A tough boss does not want to personally demean and humiliate subordinates. It's about holding employees accountable for legitimate business or organizational goals.

TOUGH BOSS versus BULLY BOSS

Tough Boss

- Acts in the best interests of the company.

- Straightforward communications.

- Clearly defined roles and tasks.

- Self-controlled and professional demeanor.

- Collaborative.

- Common and shared objectives.

- Open conflict and discussion.

- Occasional clashes.

Bully Boss

- Acts without regard to the best interests of the company or against the best interests of the company.

- Evasive communications

- Ambiguity.

- Unpredictable fits of anger and rage.

- Uncooperative.

- Long lasting, systematic unethical actions.

- Covert actions and denial of conflict.

- Always on the attack.

* *Source:* World Health Organization, *Differences between normal conflicts and mobbing,* Raising Awareness of Psychological Harassment at Work, Protecting Workers Health Series No. 4 (2003). Adapted from Table No. I.

6. EVIDENCE

"It's Not What You Know; It's What You Can Prove..." –
Denzel Washington in Training Day (2001)

Document, Document, Document...

Workers who suspect they are a target of bullying should be proactive. Bullies often work steadily behind the scenes to destroy a target's reputation through sabotage, a campaign of disparagement and a negative paper trail (warnings or poor job evaluations). Meanwhile, targets suffer potentially serious psychological and physical health injuries, depending upon the intensity and duration of the bullying. Targets of bullying often are forced out of their positions –either because they are fired, encouraged to leave, or they simply can't take it any longer.

When targets even suspect that they are being bullied, they should start gathering evidence to combat a potential adverse job action down the road – such as demotion or dismissal. If it's too late to save their job, targets still may need evidence to make a case for unemployment compensation, worker's compensation, or perhaps to file litigation against the bully and the employer.

When targets are fired, they usually cannot access a work computer. Therefore, targets should copy important employer documents while they can, including employer personnel manuals and policies. Targets also should have a copy of their job description, application, and yearly evaluations. They should copy any relevant letters, memos, e-mails, faxes, etc. from the bully and HR. This information often can be copied to a portable hard drive, a flash "jump" drive or an SD memory card. The information can be printed out later or as necessary at home. If documents are not dated, the target should date them.

Warning – if a document contains confidential information, print it out at work and black out the confidential parts before removing it from the workplace.

Targets should check the most recent version of their employee manual and other employer policy statements to determine whether the company has a policy prohibiting general workplace harassment. If the company lacks such a policy, consider suggesting that the company adopt one. If anonymity is desired, check to see if there is a venue – such as a "suggestion box" –to make the suggestion. If the company does have a general harassment policy, targets should review it carefully to understand what steps are required to formally notify the company that they are being bullied.

Often an employer designates a specific individual within a department or HR to accept complaints from workers. If and when targets are ready to complain, they should go to the designated representative and submit a detailed complaint in writing, accompanied by supporting documentation.

Targets who fail to complain or do so improperly are at risk. The employer can argue later that it should not be held liable for any damages caused by the bullying because it was never advised of the problem and was not given an opportunity to stop the bullying.

Targets also should identify possible allies, such as union representatives or supportive colleagues. This will make the road seem less lonely and allies can provide critical support if and when the target complains to HR. The target may discover that he or she is not the only one in the department who has been bullied. This is an instance where there is definitely strength in numbers.

The, target's goal should be to present a well-documented complaint to HR that creates a persuasive case supported by evidence.

Some bullies will be too savvy to provide evidence of their misdeeds. They inflict their damage in corridors when no one is looking, or behind closed doors. If targets are bullied in a verbal conversation or in private, they can still send an email to the bully restating what was said, when, and where. Keep a copy of the email and the bully's response, if any. Here's an example of a "proactive" email following a bullying incident:

> – "March 10, 2011. Hi Bob: I would like to clarify our discussion at our weekly meeting this morning. You asked me to rewrite the bible, longhand, with a quill pen, and said this assignment is due on your desk by the end of the business day. Please let me know if I have correctly

understood your instructions. If not, I would appreciate a reply email containing the correct information."

To document on-going abuse, experts recommend that targets keep a journal or small notebook, and record each instance of bullying. Ideally, the pages should be fixed – not loose-leaf – and numbered and dated. If you make an error, cross it out instead of ripping out the page, to avoid potential challenges to the journal's credibility.

Keeping a record is important because bullying usually is not a single act or behavior. Bullying is like the painting technique in which small, distinct dots of pure color are applied in patterns to form an image. Up close, one may only see dots. But, standing back and viewing the image in perspective, a clear picture can be seen. That picture is a portrait of a bully. Targets must show their employer the big picture. That may require documenting a pattern of bullying and disrespect.

A workplace-bully journal should include:

  –The date, time, place of the bullying incident and what transpired, in as much detail as possible.

  – The names of any witnesses.

  – The outcome of the event.

If a target complains to management about one incident in isolation, it is unlikely that much will change. The HR director may talk to the bully about it, and the bully might respond, "That's just what I was telling you last month. He's overly sensitive. I talk like that to everyone, and no one else complains." Or, the bully might respond, "Nothing ever runs smoothly for her. And she always has an excuse. She's the weak link that is dragging my team down."

The HR representative may be pre-disposed to believe the bully because the bully often is a member of management.

Here's another example of a journal entry:

> – 1/24/11. Bob sent me an email at 3 p.m. saying that I must accompany him to an out-of-state conference next week. I agreed, even though short notice makes it difficult to find reliable child care. I went to his office the next day to inquire about what flights he had booked so that I could book the same flights. He told me his supervisor had decided to go to the conference and that it now it was "well staffed" so I didn't have to go. I didn't go. At my job evaluation on 6/3/2011, Bob unfairly cited this incident as an example of my refusal to travel on company business.

If the target presents several well-documented instances of bullying to the Human Resources Department, there is a greater likelihood that HR will see the big picture. Of course, that doesn't mean that HR will do anything about the bully. Although times are changing, HR has not always been a safe harbor in the past for targets of workplace bullying. In fact, in many instances, the HR representative made the situation worse for the target.

Plan of Action

The target has gathered evidence to document a clear pattern of bullying. Meanwhile, of course, the target is being bullied, which can take a tremendous toll on any employee's emotional and physical health. At some point, many targets become so beaten down that they forget they have amassed years of achievement and good evaluations. They start believing that they are incompetent and worthless. They may become isolated, anxious, and fearful. Targets should not wait until their mental and physical health is compromised before taking action.

Most targets try to avoid contact with an abusive supervisor for obvious reason. This tactic, however, may increase the target's stress. A 2011 study conducted at the University of Haifa in Israel found that direct communication with a bully boss results in more positive emotions for the target than avoidance. An example of direct communication is: "I tell the supervisor directly that he/she must not treat me like that."

The study found that abusive supervision is a major organizational stressor and yet little is known about how employees cope with such stress. The study examined five types of strategies for coping with the stress factor of abusive treatment:

-Directly communicating with the abusive boss to discuss the problems.

-Using forms of ingratiation such as doing favors, using flattery and compliance.

87

- Seeking support from others.

- Avoiding contact with the supervisor.

-Reframing or mentally restructuring the abuse in a way that decreases its threat.

The most widely-used strategy reported by the 300 employees who participated in the study was avoiding contact with the abusive supervisor, disengaging from the supervisor as much as possible, and seeking support from others. The least used strategy was direct communication with the abusive supervisor — the strategy that was most strongly related to employees' positive emotions.

According to Prof. Dana Yagil, who headed the study: "It is understandable that employees wish to reduce their contact to a minimum. However, this strategy further increases the employee's stress because it is associated with a sense of weakness and perpetuates their fear of the supervisor."

Yagil says 13 to 14 percent of Americans work for an abusive boss and these workers tend to put up with workplace abuse for an average of 22 months.

While it may make the target feel better to confront the bully, it is not clear that the confrontation will make any difference in the bullying. Confronting a psychopath or an individual with psychopathic tendencies would be unlikely to help the situation and may exacerbate the abuse. Ultimately, the question of whether a target should confront a bully is a judgment call that depends upon the nature of the bully, the type of bullying involved and organization. Confrontation might be helpful if the bully seems to be genuinely unaware of the impact of his or her behavior – and is amenable to change. It also might be appropriate to confront a bully in a workplace that discourages bullying, when the bully has reason to fear repercussions if management was apprised of the problem.

In the 2011 CareerBuilder survey, nearly half of the bullied workers (47 percent) said they confronted the bully about his/her actions. Of these, 43 percent said the bullying stopped, 13 percent said the bullying became worse, and 44 percent said the bullying stayed the same.

Targets who do confront their bully are encouraged to be direct and firm. Say something unambiguous like, "I know what you're doing and I won't tolerate it. Stop it now or I will complain!" A target should document the meeting and if the bullying does not stop, include it in the target's complaint to management. Documentation showing that the target notified the bully that his or her behavior was harmful serves to put the employer on notice that the target is being bullied and made a reasonable, good-faith effort to address the problem.

After confronting a bully, targets may find some relief. But they still should closely monitor the bully's actions. It's possible that the bully has gone underground for a time, waiting for another opportunity to attack. Some experts suggest that targets make a list of the bully's aggressive behaviors and regularly review the list to see if there is any sign that the bullying has resumed. If there is any indication the bullying is continuing, then it is clear that confrontation will not solve the problem. The next step is to file a formal written and well-documented complaint in accordance with company procedures.

The Queen of Mean

Leona M. Helmsley was a successful New York City real estate investor who, along with her husband, Harry, owned a luxurious hotel chain. She was called the "Queen of Mean" because she had a mercurial temper and was said to fire employees on a whim.

She reportedly was so feared that employees throughout the Helmsley hotel empire arranged a warning system when she was en route to one of her hotels.

Despite their billions, the Helmsleys were notorious for refusing to pay contractors for work they commissioned. That behavior was the Helmsleys' undoing. Unpaid contractors revealed that work done on the Helmsley's personal 28-room mansion, was charged to their hotel chain. The couple was sued by the Internal Revenue Service for income tax evasion.

Harry Helmsley was judged to be too ill to stand trial. Not so Leona. Her trial lasted nine-weeks and was covered extensively by tabloid newspapers from around the world.

Perhaps most famously, Helmsleys' former housekeeper testified that Leona told her: "We don't pay taxes. Only the little people pay taxes."

Another witness, a former Helmsley executive, said Leona attempted to fire him several times when he refused her orders to bill work done at the Helmsley mansion to the hotel chain. (He said Harry always told him to ignore Leona and get back to work.)

Leona's lawyer presented a novel defense by arguing that Leona was a "tough bitch" who was so feared by her employees that they resorted to faking invoices on their own initiative just to minimize the time they had to spend in her company. Leona was convicted in 1989 on 33 counts of federal income tax evasion. She was fined $7.1 million and sentenced to jail – thus ending a reign of terror that cost many targets their livelihoods.

7. WHAT EMPLOYERS SHOULD DO

"One day we must come to see that the whole Jericho road must be transformed so that men and women will not be constantly beaten and robbed as they make their journey on life's highway. True compassion is more than flinging a coin to a beggar; it is not haphazard and superficial. It comes to see that an edifice which produces beggars needs restructuring." -Martin Luther King

Recognize the Problem

"My Boss's Voice Made Me Vomit!" That was the headline on a 2/15/11 story in The *New York Post*.

New York Housing Authority Superintendent Anthony Dingles had sued the Housing Authority and his boss, Demetrice Gadson, deputy director of the Housing Authority. Dingles alleged Gadson began a campaign of constant verbal attack after Dingles complained to higher ups about her poor management techniques. As a result of this abuse, Dingles said he literally became sick when heard Gadson's voice. He said the stress forced him to get medication for his stomach and intestinal system and inflamed his bleeding prostrate. He said was so beaten down emotionally that he began seeing a therapist.

The New York Post's web blog carried mocking comments about the situation: "He's obviously not married, or he'd be used to it," and "Where are the Sopranos when you need them?" The New York Post gave the incident its annual Golden Stapler "As the Stomach Turns" award. However, the story was certainly no laughing matter for the Housing Authority or New York City taxpayers. They picked up the tab for:

- Increased health costs.

- Absenteeism.

- Lost work hours, including time Dingles and Gadson spent responding to each other and time spent by Human Resources dealing with them.

-Bad publicity. The Authority was portrayed in the media as wasteful and a public laughing stock.

- Litigation costs.

Dingles filed a federal lawsuit alleging that the city, housing authority and Gadson retaliated against him for his complaints. Only the case against Gadson proceeded. After a nine-day trial, a federal jury concluded in December, 2011, that Gadson had violated Dingles' civil rights. The jury said Gadson had filed frivolous disciplinary charges against Dingles in retaliation for his complaints in violation of the First Amendment of the U.S. Constitution.

The jury sided with Dingles but it was not entirely sympathetic. The jury awarded Dingles "nominal" damages of $1. But that meant Dingles could continue working for the city. He protected his job and is no longer is supervised by Gadson.

For the city, the verdict was a disaster. Even the jury's $1 award entitled the law firm that represented Dingles to attorney fees. Such fees were expected to reach up to $450,000. This amount, of course, was in addition to the money that the city paid to defend itself, Gadson and the Housing Authority.

The employer always loses when a target of workplace bullying files a lawsuit. An employer can easily spend $100,000 to get even a lawsuit that is completely without merit thrown out. As Dingles' case showed, a lawsuit that seems to have no merit may be found to have just enough merit to become a financial disaster for the employer.

Clearly, workplace bullying can exact a heavy cost on American employers. Here are some estimates of the cost:

-"Incivility" in the workplace costs American employers about $300 billion annually, according to Christine Porath, a professor at the USC Marshall School of Business, and Christine Pearson, a professor of management at Thunderbird School of Global Management, co- authors of *The Cost of Bad Behavior: How Incivility is Damaging Your Business and What to Do About It* (2010). They say 80 percent of employees who are victims of insults or bullying in the workplace lost valuable work time worrying about the incident and 78 percent reported that their commitment to the organization declines.

– A 2007 study by the Level Playing Field Institute of San Francisco, CA, a non-profit group that promotes fairness in the

American workplace, estimates that more than two million professionals and managers in the U.S. are pushed out of their jobs each year by cumulative small comments -- whispered jokes, not-so-funny emails, etc. The Institute estimates the cost of this needless turnover at $64 billion a year.

– The Workplace Bullying Institute estimates that turnover and lost productivity due to aggressive behaviors in the workplace could cost a single Fortune 500 company as much as $24 million a year – plus $1.4 million in litigation and settlement costs.

Paging Human Resources

At its best, the Human Resources Department (HR) is a champion of ethical treatment of employees. The Code of Ethics of the Society for Human Resource Management (SHRM) exhorts HR professionals to: "Treat people with dignity, respect and compassion to foster a trusting work environment free of harassment, intimidation, and unlawful discrimination." HR departments, however, traditionally have been less than sympathetic to targets of bullying. The SHRM, which represents more than 250,000 HR professionals, opposed state workplace anti-bully legislation proposed in New York in 2010, claiming it was bad for business and unnecessary because HR professionals already address bullying issues.

In the 2011 CareerBuilder survey, 28 percent of targets said that they reported the bully to their HR department; only 38 percent said measures were taken to investigate and resolve the situation. The other 62 percent said that no action was taken. One in five targets said they didn't report the bully because they feared the bullying would escalate.

Similarly, the Workplace Bullying Institute conducted an online survey in 2009 that found that employers do nothing to correct the bully about 54 percent of the time, and actually retaliate against the complainants 37 percent of the time.

But change is afoot. In recent years, employment lawyers have begun to recommend that their clients adopt workplace anti-bully policies in anticipation of the adoption of new state legislation addressing the problem. This progress may be influenced by the fact that multi-national corporations increasingly do business in other countries where employers have a legal obligation to prevent and respond to workplace bullying. Also, there has been considerable publicity in recent years about school bullying, and some of this attention has spilled over to workplace bullying. As more employers recognize that it is in their best interest to promote a bully-free workplace, it is likely that there will be more pressure on HR to respond appropriately to complaints.

The problem of workplace bullying cannot be resolved without the cooperation of the employer. Psychiatrist Carroll M. Brodsky, in her pioneering work on bullying, *The Harassed*

Worker (1976), said workplace bullying would not occur unless the offenders felt they had the blessing, support, or at least the implicit permission of their superiors. Brodsky said organizational tolerance of bullying is communicated by the lack of sanctions against bullies who violate informal norms and values, lack of organizational policies against bullying, or both.

Other research shows that levels of bullying in a workplace reflect the organization's commitment to good people management practices. To reduce the incidence of bullying, some experts urge employers to focus on building an engaged work-team environment by:

- Involving employees in decision-making;
- Improving the quality and frequency of performance feedback;
- Establishing people-management accountability for all supervisors and managers.

Much workplace bullying could be eliminated if employers simply recognized and responded to organizational factors that encourage the problem. There may be a short-term benefit to some of these practices – such as assigning excessive work to staff - but ultimately it is contrary to the greater long-term benefits of having a committed and stable workforce. Employers may encourage bullying when they have:

- Excessive hierarchy or disinterested management;

- Inadequate staffing, which places workers under extreme pressure;
- Role ambiguity and role conflict;
- Badly defined tasks or lack of information;
- Work disorganization;
- Inappropriately short deadlines;
- Lack of employee participation in decision-making;
- Major organizational restructuring or technological change.

Perhaps the single most negligent act that any employer can commit is failing to act appropriately when presented with a bullying complaint. Inaction leaves the employer vulnerable to significant and completely unnecessary legal costs. Faced with a complacent employer targets may have no recourse but to:

- Continue to suffer emotional and physical damage until they incur a stress-related illness, which results in a claim under the state workers' compensation statute or the Family and Medical Leave Act.
- Be demoted, fired, or forced to resign (constructive termination). In the lingo of employment discrimination lawyers, this is called an adverse employment action. This can raise the stakes astronomically in litigation. (Also, the target may become eligible for unemployment benefits.)

—Consult with a plaintiff-side employment attorney to see what if anything can be done to protect the target's livelihood. A case of bullying can quickly morph into a costly legal claim alleging discrimination or retaliation.

A federal court jury in 2012 awarded a physician's assistant, Ani Chopourian, $168 million in damages, believed to be the largest judgment in history for a victim of workplace harassment in the United States. She had filed at least 18 complaints with the Human Resources Dept. during the two years she worked at Mercy General Hospital in Sacramento, CA. The record judgment includes $125 million in punitive damages and $42.7 million for lost wages and mental anguish.

Many of Chopourian's complaints involved a bullying surgeon who she said once stabbed her with a needle and broke the ribs of an anesthetized heart patient in a fit of rage. Another surgeon, she said, would greet her each morning with "I'm horny" and slap her bottom. Another called her "stupid chick" in the operating room and made disparaging remarks about her Armenian heritage, asking if she had joined Al Qaeda.

Ms. Chopourian, 45, was fired a few days after her last complaint about the doctors' demeaning behavior. A parade of witnesses, during a three-week trial, depicted a culture of vulgarity and arrogance which humiliated female employees and put patients at risk. Ms. Chopourian, who earned her physician assistant credentials at Yale School of Medicine, said administrators put up with misbehavior in the cardiac unit and the surgeons outsize egos because cardiac surgery brings in the most money for any hospital facility. "The environment at Mercy General, the sexually inappropriate conduct and the patient care issues being ignored, the bullying and intimidation and retaliation – I have never seen an environment so hostile and pervasive," she said.

An employer that ignores a workplace bullying complaint invites a target to undertake a course of action that could result in a very bad outcome for the employer. And this risk is completely avoidable when the employer had notice of the problem and had the opportunity to address it.

As previously noted, targets of workplace bullying have a tremendous amount to lose, which one reason why bullying is so devastating. With such high stakes, a target of bullying may not just fade away, especially if there are viable legal options available. From a risk perspective, it is good business sense for an employer to address and deter bullying through effective HR policies.

Be Proactive

A wise employer not only responds to workplace bullying, but strives to prevent it from occurring in the first place. This is the standard enunciated by the U.S. Supreme Court in other types of cases that involve a hostile workplace environment. In a landmark decision on sexual harassment, the Court interpreted Title VII of the Civil Rights Act of 1964 to require employers to prevent -- not simply respond to -- a hostile workplace environment.

In *Faragher v City of Boca Raton,* 524 U.S. 775 (1998), the Court ruled that an employer is vicariously liable for actionable discrimination caused by a supervisor, unless the employer exercises *reasonable care* to prevent the harassing conduct. The case involved the sexual harassment of a female lifeguard by several supervisors. The Supreme Court ruled that the city of Boca Raton failed to properly disseminate its sexual harassment policy among the supervisors and then made no attempt to keep track of the conduct of the supervisors. The Court said it was a matter of law that "the City could not be found to have exercised reasonable care to prevent the supervisors' harassing conduct."

A potential bonus of an effective workplace bully policy could be its deterrence effect on other types of bullying that are clearly prohibited by law. There is almost always some element of bullying in illegal discrimination lawsuits, including sexual harassment. Ultimately, a strong anti-bully policy could discourage litigation for other types of harassment that are currently illegal.

Employers must adopt policies and procedures to insure a work environment of mutual respect, and then follow-through by implementing the policy. Research shows that the predecessor of bullying is common workplace incivility or low-level deviant and harmful behavior. Examples of incivility are impolite behavior, snippy emails, leaving the copier jammed, the silent treatment, etc.

The motive of this kind of negative behavior may seem ambiguous. It is not always clear to all of the parties whether the incivility was intentional or unintentional. But failure to address the incivility leads to aggressive acts of bullying and violence. (*See* R. Gosh, et al., *The Toxic Continuum From Incivility to Violence: What Can HRD Do?* Advances in Developing Human Resources 13(1) 3–9 (2011).

Proper Complaint Handling

To create a respectful workplace, employers must adopt a comprehensive and multi-faceted program that includes anti-bully policies, training, leadership development, team building, communication skills training, coaching and counseling, discipline, and monitoring.

Some experts recommend a complaint procedure that involves an initial-contact person and a trained complaint resolution officer, both of whom are identified to employees in the company's anti-bully policy.

The initial-contact person is authorized to offer advice and a timely informal resolution of the matter -- if the complainant so desires. This is appropriate if it is the first incident of alleged bullying; the alleged bully has never before been accused of bullying; or if the complaint is vague, non-specific, or alleges conduct that is aggressive but appears to fall outside the parameters of the anti-bully policy. The initial contact person can clarify the anti-bully policy for the complainant, or, if the target desires, secure an agreement from the alleged bully to stop the complained-of behavior in exchange for dropping the complaint.

An informal resolution may not be suitable if complainant does not want an informal resolution or if a complaint alleges a pattern of bullying that occurs over time, is substantial and specific, and the alleged behavior clearly would be actionable under the company's anti-bully policy. (*See* discussion about the pitfalls of mediation, Chapter 8.)

If informal resolution fails - or at the complainant's request - the complaint should be forwarded to the complaint resolution officer. S/he should be a management representative who has education and training in the dynamics of workplace bullying, and who can be fair and impartial. If a complaint involves a senior management official, it may be necessary to go outside the organization and hire a trained, independent professional to handle the complaint.

Investigation

When a formal complaint is filed, the complaint resolution officer should conduct an investigation to establish the facts and the context within which the facts occurred. The officer should conduct interviews of all parties and obtain written, signed statements. It is often useful for the officer to conduct a "360 degree" or "environmental" survey of others in the department who work for and/or with the alleged bully. The officer also should examine whether there is a pattern of grievances, complaints, worker compensation claims, or unusual turnover relating to the alleged bully and/or the department where the alleged bullying took place.

The investigation should be completed within an agreed time frame, and should result in a written report containing the officer's conclusions. The report should be provided to the complainant and the alleged bully; each should have an opportunity to comment on the outcome within a specified period of time. The employer ultimately must decide what, if any, action will be taken based upon the report, the Complaint Resolution Officer's recommendations and the parties' comments. A record should be kept of the outcome of the investigation.

If the complaint is upheld, the bully should face disciplinary sanctions in keeping with company policy. If the investigator determines that the complaint was lodged for vexatious and illegitimate reasons, the complainant should face sanctions in keeping with the company policy. If the complaint is not upheld but the behavior complained of is problematic, the officer may consider engaging the alleged bully in informal management training, counseling, coaching or conduct staff trainings, as appropriate.

Both parties should have the right to appeal the final decision, and the appeal should be heard by a management official who is at the same or higher level of seniority as the complaint resolution officer. If the complainant is ultimately not satisfied with the company's actions, the complainant can file a lawsuit and a court will at some point review the process followed by the company. For this reason, it is very important to keep records and documentation.

The employer has a continuing responsibility to insure that there will be no retaliation against the complainant or any employee who provides evidence or cooperates in the investigation. More retaliation complaints were filed with the U.S. Equal Employment Opportunity Office in 2010 than complaints alleging race or sex discrimination.

Get a Policy

Experts recommend the employer assemble staff from all levels of the company to develop a specific, zero-tolerance anti-bullying policy. Common features of a workplace anti-bully policy are:

– A general statement that defines bullying. The Society for Human Resource Management suggests the following language:

[Company Name] defines bullying as repeated inappropriate behavior, either direct or indirect, whether verbal, physical or otherwise, conducted by one or more persons against another or others, at the place of work and/or in the course of employment. Such behavior violates [Company Name] Code of Ethics which clearly states that all employees will be treated with dignity and respect.

- A statement of inclusion. For example:

  This policy is meant to communicate to all employees, including supervisors, managers and executives, that X Company will not tolerate bullying behavior. The policy covers bullying at work by management, fellow employees, subordinates, clients, customers and other business contacts.

- A specific description of what is considered bullying, as well as commonplace examples. (Ex. personal insults and the use of offensive nicknames)

- A description of what is not considered bullying, as well as commonplace examples. (Ex., using disciplinary actions where appropriate)

- A description of the incident-reporting system. Such a system may include a contact person and a complaint resolution officer. The contact person receives complaints and has the authority to informally resolve minor disputes if so requested by the complainant. The complaint resolution officer handles formal complaints and is responsible for record-keeping.

- A statement encouraging the prompt reporting of bullying by targets and witnesses.

– Procedures to reduce harm to the target, possibly including opt-in, early-stage mediation at the request of the target.

– The range of potential disciplinary sanctions, up to and including the termination of the bully.

– A warning that complaints filed for vexatious or illegitimate reasons also could result in disciplinary action.

– An assurance of confidentiality for targets and witnesses who provide evidence to support the complaint.

– A prohibition against retaliation that covers both the complainant and supporting witnesses.

– An appeals process for both the target and the alleged bully. The appeal should be heard by another party with at least the same level of seniority (preferably more) than the original investigator.

– Designate a responsible person to ensure that monitoring, training, and reviews take place to prevent a recurrence of the bullying.

The policy should be widely distributed in policy and training manuals, newsletters, training courses, leaflets, websites, emails, staff meetings, and notice boards. Managers and supervisors must be trained to both prevent bullying and to address complaints speedily. Even the best policy is ineffective if it is not rigorously enforced.

Researchers on the dynamics of power say that accountability is the key to preventing workplace bullying. Power tends to reduce an individual's attentiveness to other persons' interests, feelings and expectations. Managers who understand they will be held accountable for their actions are more likely to take others' interests into account. Employers must make it clear that bullying behavior will be extremely costly to the bully. (*See* Joe C. Magee, et al., "*Leadership and the Psychology of Power*," in The Psychology of Leadership: New Perspectives and Research, edited by D. M. Messick & R. Kramer (2004))

To insure accountability, management should regularly monitor the workforce to spot signs of bullying-- such as high absenteeism, turnover, grievances, staff sabotage, failure to meet reasonable organizational goals, requests for transfers, increased disciplinary actions and increased medical costs. One effective tool to uncover hostile, toxic, or unsafe workplace issues is the anonymous employee workplace "climate" survey. Exit interviews also should be used as an opportunity to gauge the tone of the workplace environment.

EEOC's Model Policy

The Equal Employment Opportunity Commission (EEOC) enforces most of the nation's civil rights laws. It has an anti-harassment policy directed toward discrimination and sexual harassment that can also serve as a model for employers seeking to discourage workplace bullying. According to the EEOC, an effective anti-harassment policy and complaint procedure should contain:

- A clear written explanation in plain language – of prohibited conduct;

- A statement that employees who make complaints of harassment or provide information related to such complaints will be protected against retaliation;

- A clearly described complaint process that provides accessible avenues of complaint;

- A list of the officials who can receive harassment claims. It is advisable to designate at least one official outside the employee's chain of command to receive claims of harassment, because a conflict of interest could occur if the alleged harasser is within the employee's chain of command.

- Assurance that the employer will protect the confidentiality of harassment complaints to the extent possible;

- A process that provides prompt, thorough, and impartial investigation;

- Assurance that the employer will take immediate and appropriate corrective action when it determines that harassment has occurred.

- An explanation of what periodic training will be provided to all managers and supervisors regarding the terms of the anti-harassment policy and procedures, and their role in the complaint process. (Additional training for employees would also be useful.)

The EEOC also advises that the anti-harassment policy should be posted in conspicuous locations throughout the workplace, including the employer's website, and incorporated into employee orientation materials and handbooks.

OSHA's Anti-Bully Policy

The General Duty Clause of the Occupational Safety and Health Act of 1970 requires all employers to "furnish to each of his employees employment and a place of employment which are free from recognized hazards that are causing or are likely to cause death or serious physical harm...." The U.S. Department of Labor's Occupational Safety and Health Administration is responsible for implementing the OSH Act.

To date, OSHA has not promulgated national rules or enforced the OSH Act with respect to workplace bullying. OSHA did, however, recognize the serious nature of workplace bullying in 2011 when it adopted a workplace violence policy for OSHA staffers that included a strong anti-bully provision. The stated purpose of OSHA's workplace bullying policy is: "To provide a workplace that is free from violence, harassment, intimidation, and other disruptive behavior."

The OSHA policy, contained in OSHA's Field Health and Safety Manual, was drafted in cooperation with the union that represents OSHA workers, the National Council of Field Labor Locals. The anti-bully policy is contained in a chapter entitled,

"Violence in the Workplace," and defines "workplace violence" as:

> "An action, whether *verbal, written*, or physical aggression, that is intended to control, cause, or is capable of causing injury to oneself or other, *emotional harm*, or damage to property." (Emphasis added.)

The policy requires all OSHA employees to "treat all other employees, as well as customers, with dignity and respect... No employee will engage in threats, violent outbursts, intimidations, bullying, harassment, or other abusive or disruptive behaviors." Intimidating behavior is defined as: "Threats or other conduct that in any way creates a hostile environment, impair Agency operations, or frighten, alarm or inhibit others. Verbal intimidation may include making false statements that are malicious, disparaging, derogatory, disrespectful, abusive, or rude."

The OSHA policy is proactive. The policy does not spring to life when a target of bullying files a complaint. It is always in effect. It is incumbent upon management to "provide a working environment as safe as possible by having preventative measures in place and by dealing immediately with threatening or potentially violent situations." The policy also designates a management individual, OSHA's Assistant Regional Administrator/Director for Administrative Programs, with responsibility for executing the policy. The Director is required to:

– Disseminate the workplace violence policies and procedures to all employees;

– Provide annual training on this policy and U.S. Department of Labor workplace violence program for responsible OSHA Manager(s);

– Conduct an investigation and complete a Workplace Violence Incident Report for all incidents reported.

OSHA's policy can serve as guidepost for other employers on how to address the problem of workplace bullying. It also provides employees with a model of the type of policy that they can expect their employer to adopt in order to maintain a safe, bully-free workplace.

European Agreement on Harassment at Work

The 32 members and participating states of the European Union (EU) voted in 2000 to adopt The Charter of Fundamental Rights of the European Union, which states that every worker has the right to working conditions which respect his or her health, safety and dignity. The European Partners, a consortium of leading labor and business groups that negotiates EU employment policy, voted in 2007 to adopt *The Framework Agreement on Harassment and Violence at Work*. This agreement states that employers have a duty to protect workers from bullying, sexual harassment and physical violence in the workplace.

The Framework requires employers to adopt a "zero tolerance" policy and to specify procedures to be followed where cases arise. These procedures can include an informal stage in which a person trusted by management and workers is available to give advice and assistance.

According to the report, a suitable complaint procedure should:

- Protect the dignity and privacy of all. No information should be disclosed to parties not involved in the case.
- Complaints should be investigated and dealt with without undue delay.
- All parties involved should get an impartial hearing and fair treatment.
- Complaints should be backed up by detailed information.
- False accusations should not be tolerated and may result in disciplinary action.
- External assistance may help.
- If it is established that harassment and violence has occurred, appropriate measures will be taken in relation to the perpetrator(s). This may include disciplinary action up to and including dismissal. The victim(s) will receive support and, if necessary, help with reintegration.

The Framework agreement requires employers, in consultation with workers and/or their representatives, to establish, review and monitor these procedures to ensure that they are effective both in preventing problems and dealing with issues as they arise.

The EU member states are Austria, Belgium, Bulgaria, Cyprus, Czech Republic, Denmark, Estonia, Finland, France, Germany, Greece, Hungary, Ireland, Italy, Latvia, Lithuania Luxembourg, Malta, Netherlands, Poland, Portugal, Romania, Slovakia, Slovenia, Spain, Sweden, and, the United Kingdom.

Cooperating countries are: Iceland, Liechtenstein, Norway, Switzerland and Turkey.

According to the Fourth European Working Conditions Survey by the European Foundation for the Improvement of Living and Working Conditions in Dublin, Ireland, one in 20 European workers reported in 2005 that they had been exposed to bullying and/or harassment during the previous 12-months.

———

KiVa: Focusing on the Bystander

A school anti-bullying program developed in Finland in 2007 is proving to be very successful in eliminating bullying by focusing upon bystanders who witness the bullying. It could potentially serve as a model for employers seeking to eliminate workplace bullying.

The program, called KiVa, is based upon the premise that bullies are rewarded by earning higher social status because of their bullying. KiVa uses skill-building and education to empower students to defend targets, rather than to reward bullies. KiVa includes 20 hours of activities such as discussion, group work, films, role-playing, and computer exercises.

114

A large-scale 2011 study showed that in one year, KiVa halved the risk of students either bullying others or being victimized.

An interdisciplinary team of researchers at the University of Kansas plans to bring the KiVa program to American schools. A pilot program is planned in selected classrooms. If shown to be successful, the model could expand nationally.

Most bullying intervention programs either don't work or "barely work," said Todd Little, a professor of psychology and director of the Center for Research Methods and Data Analysis at the University of Kansas. "This is one of the first interventions we're seeing with effects that are impressive and pervasive," he said.

The implications for bullying in the workplace are obvious.

Could it be that bullies in the workforce also attain status by their bad behavior? Many bullies target high-achieving employees who they see as a threat to their status. By eliminating the threat, bullies protect themselves and elevate their status.

Co-workers who witness workplace bullying often fail to act or support to the target. Some bystanders fear they could be the bully's next victim while others are re-living the stress of being bullied themselves at an earlier time. Afterwards, they often feel stress and guilt for failing to intervene.

8. SPECIAL ISSUES

"Promise me you'll always remember: You're braver than you believe, and stronger than you seem, and smarter than you think." — A.A. Milne

Meditation

Many employers treat workplace bullying as they would normal workplace conflict, like a water cooler dust-up, where tempers clash and feelings get hurt. But equating normal workplace conflict with bullying is like comparing high school wrestling to professional no-holds-barred cage fighting. A bully is engaged in a pattern of coercive abuse, with the goal of vanquishing the target's spirit and, often, driving the target from the workplace. Bullying is a form of workplace violence. An employer that minimizes bullying by treating it like a mundane dispute increase the potential harm suffered by the target and, ultimately, the employer itself.

The distinction between workplace bullying and normal workplace conflict is important in several respects. The default action for many employers faced with bullying complaints is to call for mediation, which may not be appropriate in bullying cases. Mediation is almost always confidential, which helps bullies evade accountability. When mediation fails, many employers undertake

116

an investigation of the alleged bullying that may have more to do with evading liability than a search for truth.

Conflict v. Bullying

If workplace bullies used the same tactics in intimate relationships, it would be easier to identify a pattern of abuse. Bullying is on the same continuum of abuse as domestic violence and bullying supervisors use a similar palette of psychological behaviors. This can be seen by examining the *Power and Control Wheel*, a tool developed 30 years ago by domestic violence advocates in Duluth, Minnesota, to identify typical domestic violence behaviors. In the following comparison, the phrase in italics is from the Power and Control Wheel, followed by its adaptation to workplace bullying:

- *Using Male Privilege*: Instead of male privilege, abusive bosses exert "supervisory" privilege. The abusive boss alone feels entitled to define the employer/employee relationship, whether or not it bears any similarity to the target's job description. Bullies take credit for a target's work, set unrealistic deadlines, make unreasonable demands, etc.

- *Using Emotional Abuse*: Abusive bosses emotionally abuse target, putting them down, calling them names, playing mind games, etc.

- *Using Coercion and Threats*: Abusive bosses use threats of demotion or dismissal to make targets behave in ways that

117

often are unfair or demeaning (i.e. make coffee or pick up the bully's dry cleaning)

– *Using Intimidation:* Abusive bosses make targets fearful by using looks, actions and threatening gestures and by referring to weapons or physical violence.

– *Using Economic Abuse*: Abusive bosses mete out rewards and punishment as they see fit – to solidify their control – without regard to merit or actual job performance.

– *Minimizing, Denying and Blaming*: When the abuse is pointed out, the abusive boss makes light of it, minimizes it, and accuses the victim of being overly sensitive or otherwise blames the target for causing the problem.

– *Using isolation*: Abusive bosses deny targets access to professional development opportunities. They destroy the target's reputation with other managers and make it clear to a target's co-workers that the target is "unsafe." An abusive boss often signals that it is okay for others to abuse the target, a phenomenon that is called "mobbing."

– *Using Children*: Abusive bosses make targets feel guilty about letting down the company or the team. They use co-workers to relate negative messages to the target.

Because workplace bullying has many of the same dynamics as domestic violence, it is also useful to examine how society treats domestic violence. Courts around the country use mediation to tackle divorce and child custody disputes – unless the case involves domestic violence. Cases involving domestic violence automatically are diverted from the mediation track. Courts are concerned that mediation may give the abuser the opportunity to harm the victim again and that victims of abuse may not be able to adequately express or protect their own interests. Mediation is problematic for targets of workplace bullying for the same reasons.

Mediation is based upon the premise that a level playing field exists and neither party has an unfair advantage. Mediators are neutral. Their role is to assist the parties to clarify their interests and work out their own solutions. But the field is not level when one party has been abused by the other for weeks or months, and has suffered potentially serious physical and mental harm. Also, most workplace bullies are supervisors who misuse their power over subordinates, who already are in a subservient position in the hierarchy. Finally, some bullies lack empathy and will agree to a joint solution only to lie in wait, like a crocodile eyeing a shore bird, until it is safe to strike again.

Early Stage?

Mediation is more appropriate if the bullying is at a very early stage, and the mediator is educated about the dynamics of workplace bullying so he or she can call a halt to the process if it is not working as it should. Also, some targets of workplace bullying, even knowing the pitfalls, may want to give mediation a try. In that case, an employer should offer mediation that is tailored to the problems of workplace bullying. Ideally, the mediator should:

- Be independent of management.
- Be trained and/or educated about the problem of workplace bullying.
- Permit the presence of an attorney, advocate, or other third-party for the abused or vulnerable party during mediation.
- Regularly inform the parties that continuation of mediation is voluntary and that they may withdraw at any time.
- Check with the abused party between sessions to assess the party's ability to negotiate.
- Terminate mediation if the mediator believes that the abused party cannot negotiate fairly. In that case, the normal procedure for handling workplace bullying should immediately resume.
- Craft a specific and detailed agreement to reduce the opportunity for the abuser to take advantage of ambiguities.
- Include in the agreement a schedule of periodic check-backs by management with the target to insure the bullying does not resume. If it the bullying does continue, further mediation should be ruled out and the normal procedure for handling workplace bullying should begin.
- Be granted qualified immunity by the parties, prohibiting the mediator from testifying about the mediation at an employment tribunal or a court of law.

Confidentiality

One of the thorniest issues with respect to a workplace anti-bully policy is the extent to which such a policy should insure confidentiality.

Many anti-bully advocates stress the importance of insuring confidentiality to encourage targets to file complaints. They say confidentiality minimizes the target's stress and trauma and that targets might otherwise be reluctant to come forward. Targets of bullying often are ashamed or embarrassed, fearful of retaliation by the bully and concerned about being labeled a troublemaker. It is in the employer's best interest to encourage valid complaints. Problems that are unaddressed can quickly become disruptive to the functioning of the business. Also, if criminal behavior or unsafe practices are involved, a quick response can minimize an employer's potential liability.

But confidentiality comes at a price.

A down side of confidentiality is the loss of the power of the "example." When a target reports that s/he is being bullied to management, and the employer responds with a private internal procedure or investigation, other employees are left in the dark. The employer loses the benefit of the deterrent effect that occurs when workers see that managers are serious about bullying and that bullying will not be tolerated.

Silence also shields employers who are negligent or unethical. Existing and prospective employees are denied valuable insight into the nature and the extent of the problem. Often, it is not just one bully and one subordinate but a management culture that is at fault. If bullies were "outed," there certainly would be more awareness of the problem - and more pressure on the employer to address the problem.

Does it Benefit the Bully?

But perhaps the biggest problem with confidentiality is that it ultimately benefits the bully. If management decides to terminate the bully, the bully is essentially permitted to leave "to pursue other opportunities." The bully may be hired by another employer that is unaware of the bully's proclivities. The bully will have no incentive to address his or her problem, and will likely go on to bully new targets. Secrecy makes this possible.

Of course, not all bullies are unfeeling psychopaths. Some are ignorant or misguided, often because the employer failed to provide them with sufficient training in management and leadership skills. Some may not understand the consequences of their actions and might be able to make a positive change with sufficient guidance. And some alleged bullies are not bullies at all. They are falsely accused.

U.S. Securities and Exchange Commission Inspector General H. David Kotz came under fire in 2011 for allegedly instilling a climate of fear among employees in the organization. Kotz had blasted the SEC for missing the Bernard Madoff fraud, cast a spotlight on employees who viewed online pornography, and called for a criminal probe into the ethics of the SEC's former top lawyer. In his semi-annual report to Congress, Kotz questioned the SEC's decision to lease vastly more office space than the agency needs. Was Kotz a bully or was he merely holding the SEC accountable? As the SEC's internal watchdog, it was Kotz' job to investigate and report upon ethical and legal violations by SEC employees. His position was inherently vulnerable because senior officials and other powerful interests don't like being investigated or even second-guessed. Within a few months Kotz had submitted his resignation.

Not Guilty?

Not all employees who are accused of bullying are guilty. For this reason, employees who are accused of bullying are entitled (if not legally, then ethically and morally) to basic fairness and due process. They must be protected from false and malicious accusations. Like any accused, they also should have a right to be fully informed of the charge against them and to face their accuser.

Research shows that an accusation of bullying can have a devastating impact upon a manager, causing high levels of anxiety, depression and stress. (*See* M. Jenkins, et al., *Consequences of being accused of workplace bullying: an exploratory study*, 4 International Journal of Workplace Health Management, 33-47 (2011))

In some circumstances a *lack* of confidentiality can adversely impact a supervisor's career in a way that is both unfair and unnecessary. Perhaps a reasonable policy would insure confidentiality up to and until an employee who is accused of bullying is found – after a fair and just investigation – to be a bully. At that point, the bully's interests in confidentiality are outweighed by society's interest in maintaining a safe and healthy workplace. Certainly, it is not in society's best interests when an employer can pawn a bully off on a new and unsuspecting employer, where the bully can damage more lives and careers and potentially cause the new employer to incur significant damages.

Provide a Reference?

Legally, employers may be reluctant to reveal details of a bully's departure from the company to another employer out of fear of litigation. An employer that is contacted by a prospective new employer about a bully may request a copy of a release of liability signed by the bully before discussing the employee. This waiver would permit the original employer to communicate accurate information to the prospective employer, including any disciplinary action imposed in response to a complaint of workplace bullying.

When a target insists upon complete confidentiality, the employer's options are limited. As a general matter, an alleged bully is entitled to know who has filed a complaint against him or her and to respond. If a target refuses to be identified –even to the alleged bully – the employer is unable to proceed with the complaint process. Still, if an employer has reason to believe a complaint has any merit, the employer can still exercise sound judgment and be pro-active. The employer can conduct training sessions or disseminate anti-bullying information to all employees. The employer may wish to do a general "climate survey" of the bully's department to ascertain whether any other employees have concerns about bullying or the alleged bully.

An 'Independent' Investigation

Paul finally summoned up the courage to complain to the HR director about his supervisor's constant bullying. Paul (not his real name) was relieved when the HR officer was sympathetic and expressed a desire to help.

The HR officer met jointly with Paul and Paul's supervisor to help them both identify ways to improve their communications.

But it didn't take long for Paul's boss to resume his bullying ways. And now Paul has received an employment evaluation from his supervisor that is his worst in more than 20 years. Fearing the evaluation was in retaliation for his complaint, Paul complained to HR again. This time the company hired an outside "investigator" to look into Paul's complaint.

Paul spoke freely to the investigator and provided detailed evidence of bullying. He showed the investigator that his evaluation was unfair and distorted, contained factual errors, and that his boss had lied and tried to sabotage Paul's work.

A couple of weeks passed and Paul was summoned to a meeting in the office of the departmental director. The director, Paul's bully boss and the HR director were there. Paul was informed that he was being fired upon the recommendation of the outside "investigator." Paul later learned the "investigator" was an attorney hired by the law firm that represented his employer. The so-called investigator was notorious for conducting sham investigations to provide cover for employers that want to get rid of good employees who are causing problems for the organization.

Even if an investigation is fair and unbiased, targets of workplace bullying are at a disadvantage. Targets are in a defensive posture because they have the burden of proof. The inherent power differential between a supervisor and subordinate also makes it difficult for a target who is being bullied by the boss to counteract unfair evaluations, unwarranted warnings, manipulation and sabotage, and other weapons that are available to supervisors by virtue of their position.

And that's if the investigation is fair. There is no guarantee that an investigation will be fair. The investigator may be untrained and uneducated about the dynamics of workplace bullying and miss the signs of what is actually taking place. Or the so-called independent investigator may intentionally slant the investigation to achieve the best outcome for the employer.

Any employee who files a complaint of bullying should be entitled to full disclosure about the identity of the investigator, including who the investigator works for, the investigator's credentials, a statement of the specific scope of the investigation, and what the investigation will entail. The complainant should be also be informed of what steps, if any, the investigator will take to insure the investigation is fair and impartial. If that information is not forthcoming, the complainant should seriously consider whether it is in his or her best interests to cooperate in the investigation, at least without first contacting the employee's own attorney.

No HR to Complain To!

Regina works for a medical doctor, a solo practitioner, who has bullied her for several years. The practice is small and there is no human resources department to complain to.

"I have been experiencing so much emotional pain ... (It) is causing me physical problems," she says. "I am a single self-supporting female and feel like I am 'stuck' here because of the poor job market."

Regina (not her real name) says the bullying has eroded her self esteem and sense of dignity and that she is looking for another job. She says she is experiencing insomnia and panic attacks.

"They say you should never bad mouth your present employer to a potential new employer. I don't know what to say

when I'm asked 'Why do you want to leave your present job'?"
says Regina.

Anti-bully advocates often criticize HR departments for
failing to properly handle bullying complaints. What if there is no
HR department? This is the case for many professionals and small
employers. When a target complains to the boss of bullying, and
the complaint is ignored, the target may have nowhere to go except
the unemployment line.

9. STATE OF THE LAW

"Now you're not naive enough to think we're living in a democracy, are you buddy? It's the free market. And you're a part of it."- financier Gordon Gekko, Wall Street (1987).

The Big Picture

Employees have rights and protections that are rooted in contract and tort (personal injury) law, and in state and federal constitutions and statutes. However, there is considerable diversity nationally with respect to the protections accorded employees when they do not have a written employment contract or union agreement. A right or a cause of action that is available in one jurisdiction may not be available in another. This is why workers who are targets of bullying are strongly encouraged to consult an attorney in their jurisdiction.

Federal law supposedly applies uniformly across the country but, in reality, a statute may be interpreted differently in each of the 12 federal judicial circuits around the country. For example, there are differences among the circuits with respect to regulation of cyberbullying. The U.S. Supreme Court ruled in *Tinker v. Des Moines Independent School District*, 393 U.S. 503 (1969), that students retain their right to freedom of speech in schools. But schools can regulate student speech if authorities have "reason to anticipate [the speech will] substantially interfere with the work of the school or impinge upon the rights of other students." In recent years, the Second and Third Circuits have disagreed about whether off-campus cyberbullying by students of students and school staff is subject to school regulation or protected First Amendment speech. The U.S. Supreme Court declined to settle the argument last year, though it may yet.

State Laws Vary

Just as geography and climate vary between states, so do state laws. A state's law is derived from statutes adopted by the state's legislature and from the common law, the collective body of prior decisions of the state's judges. Common law guides present-day judges when they interpret laws. States are not in agreement as to whether employees can be fired without cause and they disagree about what does or would constitute just cause. Some states allow employers to fire employees who are "immoral," a vague term that is defined by the culture of the community. About half the states do allow unions to collect dues from non-members who benefit from union contract negotiations. Indiana recently became the 23rd "right to work" state, which means that unions cannot collect dues from non-union members who benefit from union contract negotiations.

The uncertainty inherent in federal and state law, and the lack of any law against workplace bullying, undoubtedly discourages targets from pursuing litigation. Conversely, the lack of any clear legal path to victory likely encourages employers to ignore or circumvent valid bullying complaints. Yet, some targets do file lawsuits and that number is increasing.

Even a decade ago, workplace bullying was hardly on anyone's radar screen in the United States. Many workers did not consider bullying to be a form of abuse. Even today some employers consider bullying to be a legitimate "tough management" style. But awareness of the problem of workplace bullying is growing as a result of the public's heightened interest in school bullying. And there has been a tremendous increase in research and scholarship on the topic, providing overwhelming evidence that workplace bullying adversely affects individuals, employers and society.

Tough to Win?

Targets of workplace bullying must now shoe-horn bullying claims into other causes of action. Researchers at DePaul University in Chicago, IL, studied cases of workplace bullying litigated in federal court from 2006 to 2008. They determined that targets prevailed in 15.6% (82 out of 524) of the cases. (*See* W. Martin, et al., *What Legal Protections Do Victims of Bullies in the Workplace Have?* J. Workplace Rights, Vol. 14(2) 143-156 (2009))

Most of the cases were based upon federal statutes like Title VII of the Civil Rights Act of 1964 and involved retaliation, harassment, and discrimination. The researchers said the cases reflected often reflected multiple claims as follows:

- Retaliation, 65.8%

- Harassment, 58.1%

- Discrimination, 52%

- Civil rights, 48.3%

- Constitutional amendments, 21.8%.

- State laws, 13.7%

- Wrongful termination, 11.8%

- Age Discrimination in Employment Act (ADEA), 9.45%

- Family and Medical Leave Act, 5.7%

- Fair Labor Standards Act/Equal Pay Act, 4.2%

- All torts, including Intentional Infliction of Emotional Distress, represented 2.2% of all cases.

Of the one in four cases that involved claims under the U.S. Constitution, most involved the First, Fourth and Fourteenth amendments. The First Amendment includes freedom of speech and assembly, and the Fourth and Fourteenth amendments pertain to due process of law and equal protection under the law, which are relevant to the issue of fairness in the termination process.

According to the researchers, 47% of the plaintiffs who won their cases filed lawsuits alleging violations of federal discrimination laws, including Title VII and the Americans with Disabilities Act. An additional 4.7 percent of the winning plaintiffs filed a claim under the ADEA. Fifteen percent of the individuals who prevailed made claims under various constitutional provisions, such as the Fourteenth Amendment's Due Process and Equal Protection clauses.

No Status?

.Of course, discrimination laws are not an option for targets who lack "protected status" on the basis of race, sex, disability, national origin, age, or religion. They have a narrower range of potential options for legal redress, including:

- The tort or personal injury claim of Intentional Infliction of Emotional Distress;
- Breach of an express or implied contract;
- The tort of Negligent Retention or Supervision;
- The public policy exception to the "Employment at Will" doctrine (ex. whistleblower retaliation).
- The Americans with Disabilities Act;
- The National Labor Relations Act;
- Speech Protections (libel, slander, invasion of privacy)
- Constructive discharge;
- Workers' Compensation;
- The Family and Medical Leave Act;
- The Fair Labor Standards Act;
- Criminal charges (battery, assault, false imprisonment, etc.)

None of these legal theories, which will be addressed in subsequent chapters, are ideal. They were not formulated to address the unique problem of workplace bullying and they touch upon only facets of the problem.

One benefit of a law that directly addresses workplace bullying would be that it provides notice to an employer that bullying will not be tolerated and could result in significant liability. A specific law also would serve as notice to workers about what types of behaviors are not acceptable in the workplace, and such a law would make it easier for workers who are targeted by bullies to find legal redress.

Where's the Civil Justice?

It must be acknowledged that even the best law and the best case would not be easy to pursue in America's troubled civil justice system.

The World Justice Institute's 2011 study of legal systems across the globe shows the United States ranks far behind other countries in providing an accessible legal system to the public. The group's report, *Rule of Law Index*, analyzed nine different factors of legal systems around the world to gauge how well they function and serve each country's residents. The U.S. ranked 21st out of the 66 countries included in the study in assuring access to the legal system. The U.S.'s lowest scores are in two areas that directly impact targets of workplace abuse - "Access to Legal Counsel" and "Access and Affordability of Civil Courts." The U.S. ranked 52nd out of the 66 countries studied with respect to affordability of legal counsel. According to the report's authors: "Legal assistance is expensive or unavailable, and the gap between rich and poor individuals in terms of both actual use of and satisfaction with the civil courts system remains significant."

Here's what many targets of bullying discover when they seek to assert their rights:

- If they can find an attorney willing to take their case, they quickly discover that many attorneys require an up-front retainer of $5,000 to $25,000 –or more – to cover anticipated costs.

- There are so many potential clients out there that some employment law attorneys say – privately at least -- they won't take a case unless a worker earns a salary of more than, say, $65,000 a year to make it worth the attorney's time.

- Funding for non-profit organizations that provide civil legal assistance to the poor has been declining for decades. Many civil legal aid programs today focus solely on legal issues of an emergency nature, such as evictions and utility shut-offs.

Where's the Fair Treatment?

If that isn't bad enough, there are specific concerns about whether employment plaintiffs are treated fairly in American courts. The win rate for employment discrimination cases is disturbingly low compared to non-jobs cases, according to Cornell Law School Professors Kevin M. Clermont and Stewart J. Schwab, authors of *Employment Discrimination Plaintiffs in Federal Court: From Bad to Worse?* 3 Harv. L. & Pol'y Rev. 103 (2009).They write that the plaintiff win rate for employment discrimination cases in federal court from 1979-2006 was 15 percent, compared to 51 percent for non-jobs cases, possibly because of hurdles placed in jobs cases that do not exist in non-jobs cases.

Clermont and Schwab say possible anti-plaintiff bias may be responsible for a 37 percent drop in the number of employment discrimination cases in federal district courts between 1999 and 2007. They say the decline may be because "federal courts disfavor employment discrimination plaintiffs, who are now forswearing use of those courts."

America's legal system places the onus on workers to protect themselves from a range of workplace abuses. For example, American workers essentially enforce civil rights laws that prohibit employment discrimination by filing lawsuits. So it is troubling that research shows American workers have a more difficult time than workers in many other countries accessing the civil justice system, and that workers in employment discrimination cases may not be getting a fair shake from federal judges who hold lifetime appointments.

Federal Approach Needed

Many workplace anti-bully advocates believe the United States should follow the lead of other industrialized countries that place the responsibility upon employers – not employees – to prevent workplace bullying. The concept of a federal leadership in this area is not revolutionary. The federal government "regulates" other kinds of workplace abuse, including exposure to industrial hazards and the failure to pay wages and benefits.

In 2012, I co-launched a national petition drive that calls upon the U.S. President and the U.S. Labor Secretary to propose national, uniform federal legislation to protect American workers from bullying. (*See* http://www.thepetitionsite.com/1/protect-us-workers/) Within just a few weeks, the petition had thousands of signatures with accompanying horror stories about workplace bullying.

There is movement in the U.S. Congress to bring at least one type of bullying under the federal purview. In 2009, for example, a federal law was proposed to address the bullying of lesbian, gay, bisexual and transgender (LGBT) students in federally-funded public elementary and high schools. By 2011, the Student Non-Discrimination Act (SNDA) had garnered has 99 co-sponsors in the U.S. House of Representatives and 27 co-sponsors in the U.S. Senate. The law is modeled after Title IX [20 USC § 1681 et seq.] of the Education Amendments of 1972. Violations would give rise to a legal cause of action for victims and could lead to loss of federal funding.

OSHA's Role?

As previously noted, a federal law already exists that should, at least theoretically, cover workplace bullying -- the U.S.

Occupational Safety and Health Act of 1970 (OSH Act). The General Duty Clause of the OSH Act requires employers to "furnish to each of his employees employment and a place of employment which are free from recognized hazards that are causing or are likely to cause death or serious physical harm to his employees...." Many studies show that high levels of stress -- such as that suffered by targets of bullying - contributes to chronic disease, including cardiovascular disease, the leading cause of death in the United States.

Susan Hartill, a law professor at Florida Coastal State University, has called upon the Occupational Safety and Health Administration (OSHA), which enforces the OSH Act, to promulgate a specific standard addressing the problem of workplace bullying. She argues that other countries have made progress dealing with workplace bullying through worker health and safety laws. Hartill says regulations are necessary because of the prevalence, high cost and devastating health impact of the problem. According to Hartill, OSHA has the "major advantage" of being an established statutory scheme with an existing regulatory apparatus.

Many other industrialized countries protect employees from workplace bullying through health and safety regulations. For example, Australian employers must "so far as is reasonably practicable" provide and maintain a working environment in which the employees are not exposed to risks or hazards. Bullying is viewed as a risk to workplace health and safety in Australia. Both employers and employees can be prosecuted for bullying. Employees can report bullying behavior to occupational health and safety inspectors, who investigate and resolve complaints. (See Joan Squelch and Robert Guthrie, *The Australian Legal Framework for Workplace Bullying*, 32 Comp. Labor Law & Pol'y Journal 15 (2010)).

Here's an actual case that demonstrates how the Australian scheme works: a worker at a radio station in Victoria, Australia, was verbally abused by a radio announcer, who had subjected fellow employees to verbal abuse and threats of violence while at work on at least time times in 2002 and 2003. The announcer also had physically assaulted a colleague. The Magistrate hearing the complaint said the "explosive manner" of the announcer in dealing with other employees was "completely inappropriate." The radio announcer was convicted and fined about $10,000 for intimidating coworkers and for failing to take care of the health and safety of others in the workplace. The broadcasting company was fined about $25,000 for failing to provide a safe workplace, about $25,000 for failing to provide instruction, training, and supervision in relation to bullying, and was ordered to pay costs.

A regulatory scheme like the one in Australia, which includes the threat of prosecution for both the employer and the employee, shows the country is serious about the problem of workplace bullying and gives employers a strong incentive to address the problem.

The Healthy Workplace Bill

Workplace bullying was virtually unknown as a societal problem in the United States until 1998, with the publication the book, *Mobbing and Emotional Abuse in the American Workplace*, by Noa Zanolli Davenport Ph.D., Ruth D. Schwartz, and Gail P. Elliott. Around this time, Ruth Namie was suffering from severe bullying in her job as a clinical psychologist. Ruth's husband, Gary Namie, a social psychologist, said the couple could find few resources in the United States to help them address the problem. In 2000, the Namies published a self-help book on workplace bullying and then established the Workplace Bullying Institute (WBI), which began a state-by-state effort to pass anti-bully legislation.

The WBI supports the proposed Healthy Workplace Bill (HWB), which is model legislation drafted by Suffolk University Law School Professor David C. Yamada. The HWB would allow targets of bullying to sue in civil court if they were subjected to a "hostile work environment," which is a term that is taken from state and federal discrimination laws.

The California legislature was the first to consider a workplace anti-bully bill in 2003 and variations of the proposed HWB have been introduced in Connecticut, Hawaii, Illinois, Kansas, Maine, Massachusetts, Minnesota, Missouri, New Hampshire, New Jersey, New York, Oklahoma, Oregon, Utah, Vermont, Washington, West Virginia, Wisconsin, Maryland,

Missouri and Montana. As of 2013, no state had approved workplace anti-bullying legislation.

Maine's legislature in 2013 adopted a very scaled down version of the Healthy Workplace Bill that was limited to a proposal to study the psychological and physical harm employees suffer due to abusive work environments. Maine Gov. Paul LePage vetoed the bill and his veto was upheld by the Maine House of Representatives in a vote of 87-56. In his veto message, the governor said the study was unnecessary because the Workers' Compensation Board already provides benefits to employees who suffer physical and psychological injuries on the job.

The New York State Senate in 2010 passed a version of the HWB by a vote of 45-16 but it subsequently died in the General Assembly.

After several unsuccessful attempts to pass the HWB in Vermont, the state senate voted in 2011 to empanel a task force to investigate "different models" to address the problem of workplace bullying on a statewide level. According to VT Senate bill S .52:

> "The Vermont Office of the Attorney General's Civil Rights Unit reports that of the 1,200 to 1,300 requests for assistance it receives each year, a substantial number involve allegations of severe workplace bullying that cannot be addressed by current state or federal law or common law tort claims. Similarly, the Vermont Human Rights Commission reports it cannot pursue complaints of workplace bullying because the inappropriate behaviors are

not motivated by the targeted employee's membership in a category protected by antidiscrimination laws."

The bill subsequently died in a Vermont House committee.

The HWB campaign involves a grassroots organizing element and has succeeded in raising awareness about workplace bullying in states where the HWB has been considered. However, the proposed HWB is far from ideal from the perspective of many workplace anti-bully advocates.

HWB Revised

Until 2013, the HWB offered far less protection to targets of workplace bullying than similar legislation adopted in other countries. Katherine Lippel, an international authority on workplace abuse, says laws in other countries do not contain the HWB's restrictive language, and that this language would make it far more difficult for an American worker to prevail in litigation. "It is understandable that the difficult context applicable in the United States with regard to rights of workers may favor a more restrictive legislative approach for purposes of political expediency, yet even some authors from the United States have expressed concern with the restrictive conditions proposed in the Healthy Workplace Bill," wrote Lippel, the Research Chair in Occupational Health and Safety Law at the University of Ottawa in Canada.

The HWB required plaintiffs to jump through hoops that are not required of plaintiffs who allege a hostile workplace environment under Title VII of the Civil Rights Act of 1964. After widespread criticism, the HWB was redrafted in 2013 to eliminate a requirement that a target prove the employer or the employee/bully acted with malice. Plaintiff's alleging a hostile workplace under Title VII are not required to show malice unless they wish to take the additional step of seeking punitive damages.

A malice requirement would be especially difficult in the context of workplace bullying because part of the "art" of workplace bullying is subtlety. And bullies are notorious for showing one face to the target and another to their supervisor – the so-called "kiss up and kick down."

The 2013 HWB, which was submitted to the Massachusetts legislature, changes a controversial requirement that targets prove they suffered "tangible" psychological or physical harm. In the 2013 bill, targets must provide "competent evidence" of "psychological harm." A similar requirement was rejected by the U.S. Supreme Court in a sexual harassment case alleging a hostile work environment because, according to the Court, the protection of federal law "comes into play before the harassing conduct leads to a nervous breakdown." (See *Harris v. Forklift Sys. Inc.*, 510 U.S. 17 (1993))

Another troubling aspect of the HWB, a $25,000 cap on damages for targets of bullying who do not suffer an adverse employment action, also was removed in 2013.

The revised HWB continues to distinguish between targets of bullying who have and have not been subjected to an adverse employment action (i.e., demotion or dismissal). The latter still cannot recover damages for emotional distress or punitive damages from the employer unless the "actionable conduct was extreme and outrageous." This limitation does not apply to "individually named defendants."

The proposed HWB allows the employer to escape liability if "the complainant employee unreasonably failed to take advantage of appropriate preventive or corrective opportunities provided by the employer." And, the HWB permits employers to present an "affirmative defense" that an adverse employment action was reasonably made because of:

-Poor performance, misconduct, or economic necessity.

- A reasonable performance evaluation; or

-A defendant's reasonable investigation about potentially illegal or unethical activity.

An affirmative defense permits an employer to argue that it should not be held liable even if all of the plaintiff's allegations are true and correct.

Hurt Feelings

Namie and Yamada have expressed concern about burdening the court system with cases that rest on "hurt feelings" rather than true bullying. They have not responded to critics who note that these concerns could apply equally to other types of cases alleging a hostile work environment, including sexual harassment or race discrimination lawsuits. Also, the U.S. Supreme Court has repeatedly said that trivial matters do not rise to the level of harm required for a hostile work environment. The Court said Title VII doesn't prohibit simple teasing, offhand comments, or isolated incidents that are not very serious. Unwelcome conduct becomes illegal when it is so severe and pervasive that it interferes with the target's work performance or creates a work atmosphere that is offensive or abusive. (*Meritor Sav. Bank v. Vinson*, 477 U.S. 57 (1986)). There is no evidence that targets of workplace bullying would flood the courts with superficial claims.

The HWB state-by-state solution appeared to have stalled in 2013. Some experts say, however, that it is just a question of time before a state approves a workplace bullying law, particularly because other industrialized countries already provide this protection to workers. Even if that happens, it will take years before a significant number of states adopt a workplace bullying law and some supposedly "pro-business" states undoubtedly never will adopt such a law. I have advocated for a national and uniform federal response to workplace bullying.

The Nevada Option

Nevada Senator Richard "Tick" Segerblom, an employment law attorney in Las Vegas, has proposed amendments to a state workplace anti-bully bill that is modeled after Title VII of the Civil Rights Act of 1964, 42 U.S.C. Sections 2000e *et seq.*, as amended. Segerblom's bill contains none of the limiting language of the HWB. It would give targets who suffer a "hostile workplace environment" the same rights as any other victim of a hostile work environment. It would eliminate the requirement that a target qualify on the basis of race, sex, religion and disability. All targets would have the right to compensatory and punitive damages, back pay, costs and attorney's fees. Segerblom introduced his bill in Nevada in 2009 and 2011 but it failed to make it out of committee both times as a result of opposition from business groups. Segerblom's bill allows employers to escape liability for bullying if they exercise reasonable care to prevent the abusive conduct and act promptly to correct the conduct.

In the absence of a national solution, some public and private employers *are* recognizing the damaging impact of workplace bullying on the targets, the workplace, and the employer's bottom line. As previously noted, OSHA adopted a strong workplace anti-bully policy in 2011 that covers its own workers. Numerous municipalities, hospitals and universities also have adopted workplace anti-bully policies. For example, the town of Canton, MA, adopted an anti-bully policy in 2010 that is applicable to all "town of Canton and Canton Public School employees, every officer including all elected and appointed town officers, all members of multiple member bodies, agents, consultants, volunteers and any person conducting business with or on behalf of the Town of Canton."

The Department of Environmental Quality for the State of Oregon in 2002 is believed to be the first public entity in the United States to approve a workplace anti-bulling policy. The

Oregon policy prohibits workplace "mobbing," which is defined as "a verbal or non-verbal conduct by one or more individuals against another individual over a period of time that continuously, systematically, and intentionally:

-Intimidates, shows hostility, threatens, offends, humiliates, or insults any co-worker;

-Interferes with a co-worker's performance; or

-Has an adverse impact on a co-worker's mental or physical well-being; or

- Otherwise adversely affects a co-worker."

Despite some hopeful signs, it appears that the state of the law with respect to workplace bullying probably will not change significantly unless and until there is a national response to the problem —which currently is not on the horizon.

10. THE HOSTILE WORKPLACE

"You gain strength, courage and confidence by every experience in which you must stop and look fear in the face."

- Eleanor Roosevelt

Title VII

Few would disagree that Bobby Wysong's supervisor at Briggs Equipment, Inc., Dallas, TX, was a workplace bully. Among other things, Mario Rodriguez blatantly referred to Wysong, who is an African-American, a "n----r," "mayate" (a racial epithet against blacks widely used in South Texas), "slave" and "dark horse." Rodriguez said he wanted the Wysong, a technician, fired -- and Wysong was fired.

There is no U.S. law against bullying. Fortunately for Mr. Wysong, however, there is a law against race discrimination– Title VII of the Civil Rights Act of 1964 (Title VII), 78 Stat. 253, 42 U. S. C. §2000e *et seq*. Title VII prohibits discrimination "with respect to . . . compensation, terms, conditions, or privileges of employment," and bans discriminatory practices that would "deprive any individual of employment opportunities or otherwise adversely affect his status as an employee."

To trigger the protection of Title VII, a target must be a member of a protected class on the basis of race, color, religion, national original and sex (including pregnancy). While federal law does not explicitly protect gays and lesbians, the U.S. Supreme Court has ruled that same-sex discrimination is actionable under Title VII. (See *Oncale v. Sundowner Offshore Servs., Inc.*, 523 U.S. 75, 80 (1998). In addition, about 20 states have extended civil rights protections to gays and lesbians.

The U.S. Equal Employment Opportunity Commission (EEOC) filed a federal lawsuit on Wysong's behalf, charging that Briggs had subjected Wysong to a racially hostile work environment. The case was settled in August 2011 when Briggs agreed to pay Wysong $112,000 in damages, and to reimburse $273,000 in medical bills from orthopedic surgery required after Wysong's wrongful termination. Briggs also agreed to provide training on Title VII to its employees.

Before a target can file a Title VII lawsuit, he or she must first file a charge with the EEOC. The EEOC may decide to investigate and prosecute the complaint on behalf of the target. (In reality, the EEOC files only 200 to 300 lawsuits a year and it has no other power to remedy a discrimination claim.) If the EEOC does not act, it will authorize the target to file a civil action on his or her own behalf in federal court.

If Wysong had not qualified for protection under Title VII, he would have had few other legal options. The Workplace Bullying Institute estimates that less than 25 percent of bullying victims have protected status under Title VII or other federal discrimination laws. That means that most targets of bullying are left to pick from a hodgepodge of common law and contract claims that are ill suited to address the problem.

Advocates of workplace anti- bullying legislation say that anyone who is subject to a hostile work environment– including the estimated 75 percent of targets who are not members of a protected class By adopting Title VII, society decreed that employees should not be required to suffer in a workplace that is hostile because of race or sex discrimination. Why should *any* worker be forced to endure a hostile work environment? There is a growing body of research showing that targets of workplace bullying suffer the same or worse emotional and physical harm as targets in discrimination cases.

Workplace bullying is not acceptable in most other industrialized countries – where employers are required to treat employees with dignity – and it should be no less acceptable in the United States.

Every state has passed state legislation that either mirrors Title VII or provides enhanced protections and penalties. State laws may be more favorable to plaintiffs than federal laws. For example, some states do not require a unanimous jury for a plaintiff's verdict and/or offer potentially larger awards, penalties and attorney fees. A state court judge also may be less likely to be thrown a workplace bully lawsuit out of court on a dispositive pre- or post-trial motion.

A disproportionate number of employment discrimination cases compared to non-job related cases are dismissed by federal judges on pre-trial or post-trial motions. In fact, some experts feel that federal judges actually "disfavor" Plaintiffs in employment discrimination cases. (*See* Kevin M. Clermont and Stewart J. Schwab, *Employment Discrimination Plaintiffs in Federal Court: From Bad to Worse?* 3 Harv. L. & Pol'y Rev. 103 (2009)). Furthermore, it appears that employers generally fare better in federal courts these days. A 2010 study commissioned by The New York Times found that the U.S. Supreme Court under the leadership of Chief Justice John G. Roberts, Jr., had ruled for business interests 61 percent of the time, compared with 46 percent in the last five years of the Court led by Chief Justice William H. Rehnquist, who died in 2005, and 42 percent by all courts since 1953.

Unwelcome Conduct

The U.S. Supreme Court first ruled in the landmark sexual harassment case, *Meritor Sav. Bank v. Vinson*, 106 S. Ct. 2399 (1986), that a "hostile environment" claim was a form of discrimination actionable under Title VII.

In *Meritor*, Mechelle Vinson, a bank teller who had been fired, said she was "constantly" subjected to sexual harassment during her four year tenure at the bank. She said bank

Vice-President Sidney Taylor coerced her to have sexual relations with him and made demands for sexual favors while at work. She said Taylor fondled her in public, exposed himself to her, and forcibly raped her multiple times. Vinson argued that such harassment created a "hostile working environment" that was covered by Title VII.

The U.S. Supreme Court agreed, ruling that a plaintiff could establish a violation of Title VII "by proving that discrimination based on sex has created a hostile or abusive work environment." The Court subsequently elaborated on the hostile workplace theory in *Harris v. Forklift Sys. Inc.*, 510 U.S. 17, 21 (1993). The Court said unwelcome conduct becomes illegal when it is so severe and pervasive that it interferes with the target's work performance or creates a work atmosphere that is offensive or abusive.

It is not easy for targets of workplace bullying to prevail in a Title VII case. Discrimination refers to the prejudicial treatment of different categories of people. The presence of bullying is often easy to spot in a discrimination complaint but the presence of discrimination can be far from obvious in a workplace bullying complaint. And even when discrimination exists, it may not be decisive in a workplace bullying complaint if it is not pervasive.

Hostile Environment Defined

Workplace bullying *per se* does not violate Title VII unless it is accompanied by illegal discrimination on the basis of race, sex, etc. So it is necessary to look at Title VII discrimination cases that involve bullying to understand the meaning of a hostile workplace environment in that context.

The EEOC said the central inquiry in a Title VII sexual harassment case is whether unwelcome conduct rises to the level of a hostile environment. Is the environment sufficiently severe? Does the conduct "unreasonably interfere with an individual's work performance" or create "an intimidating, hostile, or offensive working environment." 29 C.F.R. § 1604.11(a) (3). When the alleged conduct is non-physical – as it often is in workplace bullying situations – the EEOC examines the nature, frequency and context of the remarks. Relevant questions to this inquiry, according to the EEOC, are whether the target was singled out for abuse; the relationship between the target and the harasser; and whether the remarks or conduct were hostile and derogatory.

There is no clearly delineated boundary line between incivility in the workplace and bullying. The U.S. Supreme Court stated in the landmark sexual harassment case, *Meritor Sav. Bank v. Vinson,* that the "mere utterance" of an ethnic or racial epithet which engenders offensive feelings in an employee would not affect the conditions of employment to a sufficiently significant degree to violate Title VII. Plainly, more than a mere utterance is required. But how much more?

The U.S. Court of Appeals in the Second Circuit offered guidance in its widely-cited decision, *Alfano v. Costello,* 294 F.3d

365, 373 (2d Cir. 2002). The appellate court said a hostile work environment must be "so severely permeated with discriminatory intimidation, ridicule, and insult that the terms and conditions of [the victim's] employment were thereby altered." Normally an isolate incident or episodic incident would be insufficient unless it was sufficiently severe if it "work(s) a transformation of the plaintiff's workplace...."

In *Alfano*, the Court held that the Plaintiff failed to provide sufficient evidence at trial to establish a hostile work environment under Title VII. Georgiann E. Alfano was hired by the New York Department of Prisons to work as a guard in a medium security prison housing 2,000 male prisoners. She cited four humiliating incidents stemming from a conversation with a prison captain who said a lieutenant had seen Alfano simulating oral sex with a carrot in the prison dining area. The captain told Alfano to stop eating carrots, bananas, hot dogs and ice cream on the job a "seductive" manner. A trial court jury found in favor of Alfano on the hostile work environment claim and awarded her $150,000 in compensatory damages for emotional distress.

The Court conceded that Alfano's conversation with the captain was "objectionable" but said the subsequent incidents were perpetuated anonymously, making it difficult for the employer to address. "A reasonable person could have found the carrot and cartoon incidents humiliating, and they were plainly offensive. But they were too few, too separate in time, and too mild, under the standard so far delineated by the case law, to create an abusive working environment," said the Court.

A single incident of harassment was found actionable by the Eighth Circuit Court of Appeals in *Barrett v. Omaha National Bank*, 726 F.2d 424 (1984). In that case, the plaintiff was sexually harassed by a supervisor who talked to her about sexual activities and touched her in an offensive manner while they were inside a vehicle from which she could not escape.

According to the EEOC, a violation is more likely to be found when the target is subject to both verbal and physical conduct. The EEOC states that a plaintiff alleging a hostile work environment must demonstrate either that a single incident was extraordinarily severe, or that a series of incidents were sufficiently continuous and concerted to have altered the conditions of her working environment.

A Title VII Analysis

Here are some preliminary factors to consider when evaluating whether a target has a discrimination claim:

1. Was the target discriminated against because of his or her membership in a protected class on the basis of race, color, national origin, religion, or sex (including pregnancy)?

2. Is the employer covered? Title VII applies to employers with "fifteen or more employees for each working day in each of twenty or more calendar weeks in the current or preceding calendar year." 16 42 U.S.C. § 2000e (b). This

includes state and local governments, employment agencies, labor organizations, and the federal government. But certain employees are not covered, including some who work for religious institutions and certain businesses on or near a Native American reservation.

3. Was the illegal discrimination sufficiently severe to support a Title VII? It must be pervasive enough to alter the conditions of employment and create an abusive working environment.

Not a "civility" code

Targets of workplace bullying face two major obstacles in a Title IX case. They must show the abuse was sufficiently severe or pervasive to transform the target's working conditions and they must show the abuse was motivated by discrimination. The U.S. Supreme Court has made it more difficult for plaintiffs to prevail in these types of cases through decisions that caution federal courts to refrain from serving as the ultimate arbiter of employer personnel decisions.

The Court said that Title VII is not meant to be a general "civility code" for the workplace, and should only reach illegal discrimination on the basis of race, sex, religion, national origin, etc. (See *Oncale v. Sundowner Offshore Serv., Inc.*, 523 U.S. 75, 80 (1998)). Furthermore, the Court said that Title VII does not prohibit simple teasing, offhand comments, or isolated incidents that are not serious. Generally, a lone insulting comment or epithet directed at a worker's race, sex or religion in the midst of a campaign of bullying will not be enough to support a Title VII claim.

The essence of workplace bullying often is repeated demeaning and humiliating actions that when viewed independently tend not to appear very serious, but taken together show a devastating pattern of abuse. Workplace bullying typically includes random insults, casual slurs, withholding needed information from assignments, usurping credit for the target's work, isolation, undeserved criticism behind closed doors, threats of dismissal, etc.

In reality, the difference between bullying and incivility is the difference between no-holds-barred cage fighting and a Sunday afternoon fencing demonstration. Incivility implies a breach of good manners and a lack of courtesy whereas bullying involves intentional abuse, repeated over time. But the Courts' admonition in *Oncale* sent a signal to lower courts; they are expected to serve as gatekeepers − to keep the courthouse doors closed to all but the most egregious discrimination-based, hostile workplace environment complaints.

The Supreme Court further stated in *Oncale* that Title VII does not include "genuine but innocuous" differences in the ways men and women routinely interact with members of the same or opposite sex. The Court said the conduct in question must be severe enough "to ensure that courts and juries do not mistake ordinary socializing in the workplace-such as male-on-male horseplay or intersexual flirtation for discriminatory 'conditions of employment.'"

The plaintiff in *Oncale* was a 21-year-old roustabout on an oil rigger in the Gulf of Mexico, Joseph Oncale. He complained of sex discrimination by three male co-workers who forcibly subjected him to humiliating sex-related actions in the presence of other crew members. He said two of the co-workers physically assaulted him in a sexual manner, and another threatened him with rape. Oncale complained to the company's safety compliance clerk. The clerk's only response was to say that Oncale's tormentors also "picked [on] him all the time too" and that they called him (the clerk) a name suggesting homosexuality.

Lower courts rejected Oncale's sexual harassment complaint on the grounds that Title VII was not intended to address same-sex harassment. But the U.S. Supreme Court unanimously disagreed. The Court said recognizing same-sex harassment would *not* transform Title VII into a "general civility code" for the American workplace. The Court also said that the critical issue in Title VII is whether members of one sex are exposed to disadvantageous terms or conditions of employment because of sex – and not necessarily by the opposite sex.

The *Oncale* decision sheds light on the degree of severity of behavior that is considered sufficiently hostile and pervasive. It would not be harassment, the Court said, if a professional football coach smacked a professional football player on the buttocks as the player exited the locker room to enter the playing field. The same behavior, the Court said, would be abusive if directed at the coach's secretary (male or female) back at the office. Ultimately, the Court said, whether behavior is actionable must be judged from the perspective of a reasonable person in the plaintiff's position, considering all the circumstances.

Judicial Vagaries

Most targets of workplace bullying would empathize with Joseph Clark, 51, a retail auto parts specialist who was called "old cripple" by a contentious 29-year-old co-worker. The young man also threatened to physically harm Clark on several occasions. Nevertheless, a federal judge in Arkansas dismissed Clark's complaint of age and disability discrimination. (*Clark v. O'Reilly Auto. Inc.*, No. 09-00851 (E.D. Ark, 5/23/11). The Court said Clark -- who suffered from lupus, fibromyalgia, diabetes, and arthritis -- had not shown that his hostile work environment was sufficiently severe.

"[E]ven if Clark could show that Hanson routinely called him names like 'cripple' and 'old man' it would not meet the rigorous standard for hostile work environment claims because simple teasing, offhand comments, and sporadic use of abusive language do not materially alter the terms and conditions of employment," said the Court.

There was a different result in an Arizona case involving alleged sexual harassment, *Pappas v. J.S.B. Holdings Inc.*, 392 F. Supp. 2d 1095 (D. Ariz. 2005).

A female quality assurance manager said she quit after being bullied for six months by three men working in the engineering department of an aerospace company. The men did not report to her, she said, but resented her higher salary and her promotion. She said they made offensive remarks related to her gender, gave her dirty looks, tampered with her computer, stapled her business cards together, bumped into her repeatedly, drew a mustache on a picture of her grandson in her cubicle, and falsely accused her of giving obsolete specs to a co-worker. She said she left the job after she began to shake uncontrollably when the men walked into her department

A federal judge refused to dismiss the complaint, despite finding that almost all of the specific instances of "aggravating and antagonistic conduct" about which the plaintiff complained were "on their surface neither sexual in nature nor gender directed." Citing earlier decisions, the Court said "non-sexual" conduct can be illegal sex-based harassment if it is shown that "but for" the employee's sex, he or she would not have been the subject of harassment.

The Court said the use of certain misogynistic terms by the plaintiff's co-workers might permit a jury to conclude that the plaintiff was subjected to a hostile work environment at least in part because of her gender. Furthermore, the Court said that a jury could conclude that the employer was liable for damages because the harassment continued for months after the plaintiff complained, and no disciplinary action was taken against the harassers.

The Court also refused to dismiss the plaintiff's claim that she was a victim of retaliation, ruling that a reasonable person could find she was subject to constructive dismissal, constituting an adverse employment action for asserting her rights under Title VII.

The Undiscriminating Bully

A common problem encountered in workplace bullying cases involves the issue of whether the target was singled out for mistreatment. Is the bully abusive to everyone who works for him or her? If so, it's probably not discrimination.

Sadly, in the United States, employers essentially are free to mistreat employees as long as they do not single out members of a protected group and treat them differently. In other words, it is okay to be an "equal opportunity" bully. Such was the case in *Street et al v. U.S. Corrugated Inc*, No. 1:08-cv-00153, (W.D. Ky. 2011).

Five employees, two males and three females, were fired after they complained to management about their abusive supervisor. The company's defense was that the supervisor was equally abusive to all employees, and therefore his actions were not discriminatory.

U.S. District Judge Joseph H. McKinley dismissed the plaintiffs' Title VII claims of sex discrimination and retaliation. Judge McKinley conceded that the supervisor, Robert Greathouse, often yelled, used profanity, threw objects, made physical threats, and was generally difficult to work with. However, Judge McKinley said Greathouse mistreated subordinate employees regardless of gender and therefore was not engaged in an unlawful action.

"Title VII only protects employees from retaliation for having opposed an employer's unlawful actions, such as discrimination based on gender, age or race. There is no protection under the act for employees who simply complain about the boss being a bully," said Judge McKinley.

No One is Safe?

Judge McKinley also dismissed the employees' state law claims, including breach of contract, terroristic threats, and intentional infliction of emotional distress. The terroristic threat claim stemmed from the following exchange between Greathouse and one of the plaintiffs:

Greathouse: "I brought my big guns in today."

Filback: "Well I guess I'll hide under my desk."

Greathouse: "You're not safe there. No one is safe."

Judge McKinley said "no reasonable juror" could possibly conclude that Greathouse's statements amount to a terroristic threat. In a footnote to his opinion, Judge McKinley acknowledged that Greathouse allegedly left a gun on an employee's desk. He noted, however, that the employee in question was not a party to the lawsuit.

It was perhaps some comfort to the unemployed plaintiffs that the company removed Greathouse from his supervisory job after receiving their complaints.

Even a bully who appears to treat all subordinates badly may in fact be judged to have treated some worse than others for discriminatory reasons. The U.S. Court of Appeals for the Ninth Circuit said in *EEOC v. Nat'l Educ. Ass'n*, 422 F.3d 840 (2005), that the harassing behavior of an Alaska teachers' union official supported an inference of sex discrimination even though the union official abused both female and male employees. The Court said the man was especially obnoxious towards his female subordinates, often screaming profanities and physically intimidating them, while treating his male subordinates in a more playful, bantering fashion. "Offensive conduct that is not (on its face) sex-specific nonetheless may violate Title VII if there is sufficient circumstantial evidence of qualitative and quantitative differences in the harassment suffered by female and male employees," said the Court.

Merely Humiliating

The fine line between bullying and discrimination was tested in the Louisiana case of *Love v. Motiva Enters. LLC*, No. 08-30996, unpublished opinion (5th Cir. 10/16/09). The U.S. Court of Appeals for the Fifth Circuit, in a 2-1 decision, upheld the dismissal of a sexual-harassment complaint on the grounds that the plaintiff had merely proven humiliating or bullying behavior. The

Court said to prevail in a sexual harassment claim a plaintiff must establish that the alleged conduct was not merely tinged with offensive sexual connotations but actually constituted sex discrimination.

The case involved allegations by Connie M. Love that a co-worker, Jeanne Sirey, called her offensive names, twice touched her under her underwear, and made other unwanted physical contact, such as trying to hug Love and repeatedly rubbing her breasts against Love. The Court said the incidents did not support "an inference of sexual attraction and implicit proposals for sex in light of Sirey's consistent insults toward Love and demonstrated negative feelings about Love and her appearance... Sirey's conduct is more indicative of humiliating or bullying behavior." The Court also said Sirey was "rude and obnoxious" to all of her co-workers generally.

Based on these mixed rulings, it is obvious that Title VII is not a panacea for targets of workplace bullying. But even targets who lose their discrimination claim might be able to prevail against an employer. Title VII offers two bites of the proverbial apple. Not only can Plaintiffs sue for discrimination under Title VII, but Plaintiffs also can sue employers who retaliate against them for complaining about discrimination.

Retaliation

A record number of employment discrimination charges were filed with the U.S. Equal Employment Opportunity

Commission (EEOC) in 2011 The largest single category of complaints involved retaliation. Of 99,947 charges of employment discrimination in Fiscal 2011, the EEOC received 37,334 complaints of retaliation, which represents 37.4 percent of all charges filed in 2011.

All of the laws enforced by the EEOC, including Title VII, make it illegal for an employer, employment agency or labor organization to fire, demote, harass, or otherwise "retaliate" against people (applicants or employees) because they engaged in protected activity.

Perhaps responding to the sharp rise in retaliation claims, the U.S. Supreme Court in 2013 issued a ruling in *University of Texas Southwestern Medical Center v. Nassar* that makes it far more difficult for plaintiffs to prevail in these types of cases.

The plaintiff, Dr. Naiel Nassar, a physician, said he was denied a faculty position with a University of Texas medical center because he complained he was the victim of discrimination on the basis of his Middle Eastern background.

In a 5-4 ruling, Justice Anthony M. Kennedy, writing for the majority, said the plaintiff must show the retaliation would not have occurred "but for" the defendant's discriminatory conduct. In the past, it was sufficient to win if the plaintiff could show that retaliation was a motivating factor for an adverse employment action (demotion, dismissal, etc.).

It is a rare case that an employer cannot point to at least one other factor to justify an adverse employment action.

Justice Kennedy cites the Court's somewhat notorious ruling in an age discrimination case (See *Gross v. FBL Financial Services, Inc.*, 557 U. S. 167, 176.) The Court distinguished the Age Discrimination in Employment Act of 1967 from other types of discrimination cases by requiring plaintiffs to prove that age discrimination was the "but for" cause of an adverse employment action.

In *Nassar*, the majority said it would be "inconsistent' with the structure and operation of Title VII to permit a lower standard of proof and thus raise the costs, both financial and reputational, on an employer whose actions were not in fact the result of any discriminatory or retaliatory intent.

In her dissent, Justice Ginsburg wrote, "The ball is once again in Congress's court to correct the error into which the court has fallen and to restore the robust protections against workplace harassment the court weakens today."

Protected Activity

The law forbids retaliation in any aspect of employment – including hiring, firing, pay, job assignments, promotions, layoff, training, fringe benefits, and any other term or condition of employment. The law even applies to past employees. For example, an employer cannot give a former employee a negative job reference in retaliation for filing an EEOC charge against the employer.

Protection from retaliation also extends to individuals who "oppose" a practice made unlawful by one of the employment discrimination statutes. For example, Dick complains that a supervisor is sexually harassing a co-worker, Jane. Both Dick and Jane are fired. Either or both Dick and Jane file a retaliation claim. A person needs only a good faith and reasonable believe that the opposed practices were unlawful to be protected against retaliation. It doesn't matter if the individual was incorrect in his or her belief, and the practices ultimately are deemed to be lawful.

Protected activity also includes filing a charge, testifying, assisting, or participating in any manner in an investigation, proceeding, or hearing under the applicable statute.

The scope of actionable retaliation was expanded in 2011 to include claims made by "associates" of employees.

In a unanimous decision, the U.S. Supreme Court, in *Thompson v. North A. Stainless, LP*, 130 S. Ct. 3542 (2011), ruled that if an employee files a claim of employment discrimination, and another employee who is a close family member of the complaining employee suffers an "adverse employment action," this may be considered retaliation.

Eric Thompson was fired by North American Stainless (N.A.S.) because his fiancée, Miriam Regalado, filed a discrimination claim against the company. According to the Court: "... accepting the facts as alleged, Thompson is not an accidental victim of the retaliation. Hurting him was the unlawful act by

167

which NAS punished Regalado. Thus, Thompson is a person aggrieved with standing to sue under Title VII."

The Supreme Court said Title VII's anti-retaliation provision covers a broad range of employer conduct which prohibits any employer action that would dissuade a reasonable worker from making or supporting a discrimination charge. The Court notes that "a reasonable worker obviously might be dissuaded from engaging in protected activity if she knew that her fiancé would be fired."

While courts generally accept an expansive definition of retaliation, they also have ruled that a worker's manner of opposition to alleged unlawful discrimination must be reasonable. It is *not* reasonable for an employee to photocopy confidential documents relating to alleged discrimination and to circulate those documents among co-workers, or to make threats of violence to life or property. Courts have found that a work slowdown, or even public criticism such as peaceful picketing, is reasonable.

Employees have lost many important cases before the U.S. Supreme Court in recent years. A recent study published in the Minnesota Law Review determined that the Court is the most pro-business Court since World War II.

Until the Nassar ruling, a plaintiff in a discrimination case could lose on the merits of their lawsuit and still win a retaliation claim.

A case in point was *Mendez v. Starwood Hotels & Resorts Worldwide, Inc.*, 2010 U.S. Dist. LEXIS 107709 (S.D.N.Y. Sept.

30, 2010). After a three-week trial in 2010, a federal jury in New York rejected Moises Mendez' claims of discrimination based on national origin (Ecuadorian) and race (Latino) and disability (diverticulitis and diabetes). But the jury found in Mendez' favor on a single claim of retaliation. The defendant, Starwood Hotels & Resorts Worldwide, Inc., was ordered to pay Mendez $1 million in compensatory damages and $2 million in punitive damages.

The jury said that Mendez – who was employed at the Westin Times Square branch of the hotel management chain – was a victim of retaliation after he complained about discrimination. Management installed a hidden camera above Mendez' work station, where it remained for eight days until co-workers found it and disabled it. The jury rejected the hotel's claim that the camera was installed to help management investigate Mendez's complaints about vandalism at his work station and locker.

Mendez' award later was drastically reduced on appeal by U.S. District Judge Colleen McMahon. "The court is convinced that the jury felt sorry for plaintiff—as, indeed, the court felt sorry for the plaintiff," said Judge McMahon, adding, "Mendez endured an abusive workplace and got very little sympathy or assistance from either his employer or his union." Judge McMahon speculated that the jurors were searching for a way to hold the employer liable and their award was "in proportion to the teasing and rudeness Mendez endured at the hands of his fellow workers and chefs…."

Mendez ultimately received only $10,000 in compensatory damages and $300 in punitive damages. The litigation, however, likely cost Starwood millions of dollars when its court costs and fees (include Mendez' attorney fees) were tallied up.

Link between Bullying and Discrimination

There is an element of bullying in almost any type of discrimination case. If employers had effective policies in place to discourage bullying, it is quite possible that they would face fewer race and sex discrimination lawsuits.

Bigotry, for example, is characterized by prejudice and intolerance and is often expressed in bullying behaviors. A bully who is biased against minorities may use humiliation and isolation to express bigotry.

The Center for American Progress estimates that American employers pay $64 billion a year for workplace discrimination – which is the annual estimated cost of losing and replacing more than 2 million American workers who leave their jobs due to unfairness and discrimination. This does not even include litigation costs, absenteeism, lost work time, increased health care costs, etc.

Retaliation claims may be skyrocketing because they are easier to prove than a substantive claim of discrimination. Targets need only show that:

- They filed of a claim or complaint of discrimination;
- They suffered an "adverse employment action" by the employer;

-There was a causal connection between their complaint and a subsequent adverse employment action.

At that point, the burden shifts to the employer to show that it had a legitimate nondiscriminatory reason for the adverse employment action. Compared to the twists and pitfalls of proving a discrimination claim, a retaliation claim may be a relatively easy win. Other federal discrimination statutes that contain an anti-retaliation provision include the Family and Medical Leave Act; the Equal Pay Act; the Age Discrimination in Employment Act; the Americans with Disabilities Act.

The BFOQ Defense

Title VII permits an employer to consider discriminatory factors when making employment decisions if they are "reasonably necessary to the normal operation of the particular business or enterprise." The "bona fide occupational qualifications" (BFOQ) exemption or defense applies in cases involving religion, sex, and national-origin discrimination. Basically, the employer concedes that it discriminated against the worker but says the discrimination was necessary.

In *Everson v. Michigan Dept. of Corrections*, 391 F.3d 737 (6th Cir. 2004), the Court held that being "female" was a BFOQ for certain correctional officer positions. Due to problems with sexual assaults and invasion of privacy of female inmates, the Michigan Department of Corrections (MDOC) decided that approximately 250 positions of Correctional Officer and

Residential Unit Officer in the housing units of female prisons should be "female only." The plaintiffs brought suit alleging violations of Title VII and Michigan state law. A court found in favor of the plaints, but the appeals court ruled that the MDOC met the requirement of the BFOQ defense and reversed the lower court's finding.

The appeals court said gender-based discrimination is countenanced in certain instances where sex is a bona fide occupational qualification reasonably necessary to the normal operation of that particular business or enterprise. The Court concluded, however, that the BFOQ defense is proper only where:

- An employer has a basis in fact for its belief that gender discrimination is reasonably necessary -- not merely convenient -- to the normal operation of its business.
- A job qualification that requires discrimination must be related to the essence or to the central mission of the employer's business.
- The employer has the burden of establishing that it had no reasonable alternatives to discrimination.

The Court said it was "simply holding that given the endemic problem of sexual abuse in Michigan's female facilities, given the constellation of issues addressed by the MDOC's plan (security, safety, and privacy), and given the deference accorded the MDOC's judgment, the MDOC's plan is reasonably necessary to the normal operation of its female prisons."

The Faragher/Ellerth Defense

It is critical that targets follow the dictates of their employer's anti-harassment policy when reporting workplace abuse. An employer can advance an affirmative defense in a Title VII sexual harassment claim involving a hostile work environment. Known as the *Faragher/Ellerth* defense, the employer can escape liability for damages if:

- The employer "exercised reasonable care to prevent and correct promptly any sexually harassing behavior," *and*
- The plaintiff employee "unreasonably failed to take advantage of any protective or corrective opportunities provided by the employer or to avoid harm otherwise."

If an employee complains about discrimination and management does not respond appropriately, the company may lose its *Faragher/Ellerth* affirmative defense.

The Seventh Circuit Court of Appeals ruled in a 2012 Wisconsin case involving a hostile workplace claim that even the best policy won't protect an employer if it is not followed. The case, *EEOC v. Management Hospitality of Racine, Inc., et al.,* No. 10-3247 (7th Cir. Jan. 9, 2012), involved two teens who worked at an IHOP restaurant operated by the defendant. Both complained to managers that they were being sexually harassed by the same assistant manager, but the company did not respond. In fact, the company did not begin investigating the complaints until a private investigator hired by an attorney for one of the teenager began asking questions.

The Court ruled that the *Faragher/Ellerth* affirmative defense was not available to Management Hospitality, even though the company (which operates 21 International House of Pancakes restaurants) had a "zero-tolerance" anti-harassment policy in place, conducted some anti-harassment training and had a policy of investigations of complaints. The Court said "the mere creation of a sexual harassment policy will not shield a company from its responsibility to actively prevent sexual harassment in the workplace."

The Court concluded that a rational jury could have found that the sexual harassment occurred "every shift" was "highly offensive," and included "physical touching." In addition, the Court said, a rational jury could find that the employer failed to follow its own policies because it discouraged employees from reporting complaints, provided inadequate anti-harassment training to supervisors, and failed to "promptly" investigate the complaints.

The EEOC filed suit on behalf of the two teenaged servers. A jury awarded one of the servers $1,000 in compensatory damages and the other, $4,000 in compensatory damages. In addition, the jury found that the IHOP had acted recklessly with respect to one of the servers and awarded her $100,000 in punitive damages.

Title VII's Coverage

As noted, Title VII generally applies to employers with 15 or more employees, employment agencies, and labor organizations engaged in an industry affecting commerce. Exemptions from Title VII coverage, in whole or in part, include:

- Religious corporations, associations, educational institutions, or societies employing individuals of a particular religion.
- Bona fide, tax-exempt private clubs.
- Native American tribes and businesses on or near a Native American reservation that give preferential treatment to individuals living on or near the reservation.
- Aliens employed outside the United States.
- Civilian employees of the Army, Navy, and Air Force and not uniformed military personnel.

The federal government and departments or agencies of the District of Columbia that are subject to procedures of the competitive service are excluded from the definition of "employer" but they are separately covered under Section 717 of Title VII (42 U.S.C. § 2000e-16).

Summary: Title VII

Who is eligible: A member of a "protected" class. A person who is the victim of discrimination on the basis of race, sex (including pregnancy) national origin, color or religion. In general,

175

the employee must work for employers with 15 or more employees.

Major provisions: Title VII prohibits discrimination or harassment – on the basis of sex, national origin, color or religion – with respect to the hiring, firing or any term or condition of employment.

Damages: Back pay and/or front pay; compensatory damages; reinstatement; punitive damages; attorneys' fees.

For more information, go to the Equal Employment Opportunity Commission at http://www.eeoc.gov/.

11. EDUCATIONAL INSTITUTIONS

"To go against the dominant thinking of your friends, of most of the people you see every day, is perhaps the most difficult act of heroism you can perform.'

- Theodore H. White

Title IX

Another federal law that addresses workplace abuse is Title IX of the Education Amendments of 1972 (*See* 20 U.S.C. § 1681-1688 (2006), which prohibits public and private schools that receive federal financial assistance from discriminating on the basis of sex. Both students *and employees* are covered by Title IX. Schools that violate Title IX can face administrative remedies, lose their federal funding, and be sued civilly for damages or injunctive relief. Title IX provides that:

> "No person in the United States shall, on the basis of sex, be excluded from participation in, be denied the benefits of, or be subjected to discrimination under any education program or activity receiving Federal financial assistance …" (20 U.S.C. Section 1681(a))

Title IX is best known for requiring parity between the sexes in athletics programs offered in high schools and colleges but the law goes far beyond that. Title IX covers, among other things, admissions, recruitment, financial aid, academic programs, student treatment and services, counseling and guidance, discipline, classroom assignment, grading, vocational education, recreation, physical education, athletics, housing, and employment. In recent years, Title IX has been successfully invoked to combat the bullying of students.

The U.S. Supreme Court ruled in *Davis v. Monroe County Board of Education*, 526 U.S. 629 (1999), that a school board can be liable under Title IX for responding with deliberate indifference to student-on-student sexual harassment if it has actual knowledge of the harassment. The Court said the harassment must be "so severe, pervasive, and objectively offensive that it can be said to deprive the victims of access to the educational opportunities or benefits provided by the school."

The *Davis* case involved a 5th grade student, LaShonda D., who was harassed over a five-month period by G.F., a fifth grade male student. School officials ignored repeated complaints by LaShonda and her parents, failed to discipline G.F., and, in one class, would not even relocate LaShonda's desk, which was next to G.F's desk. LaShonda's father filed a Title IX lawsuit after he found a suicide note written by LaShonda.

The Supreme Court held that "when school officials respond with deliberate indifference to a known sexually hostile or abusive environment in an education program or activity, they subject the harassed student to that environment in violation of

Title IX, whether the harasser is a school employee or another student," The Court said the educational institution is not responsible for the acts of the harassing individuals but for its own actions or inaction when it became aware of the harassment.

The Davis case applies explicitly to the bullying of students, and the law views students and adults very differently. Yet, Title IX applies to employees as well as students. It remains to be seen whether Title IX can be successfully employed to combat workplace bullying by teachers and staff.

Minnesota's largest school district entered into a comprehensive settlement agreement in 2012 with two federal agencies that had sued the district for failing to protect lesbian, gay and transgender (LGBT) students from bullying and harassment. Under the settlement, the U.S. Dept. of Justice (DOJ) and the U.S. Dept. of Education's Office of Civil Rights (OCR) will monitor the Anoka-Hennepin School District until 2017.

Federal authorities began investigating the district in 2010 after receiving a complaint that it had failed to adequately address peer-on-peer harassment on the basis of sex and sexual orientation. Six students said they faced a constant torrent of anti-gay slurs due to their actual or perceived sexual orientation. They said they were choked, shoved, urinated on and even stabbed with a pencil. The students charged that an 18-year-old "gag rule" adopted by the district hampered the efforts of teachers to end the harassment and stigmatized gay and lesbian students. The policy required staff to stay neutral on LGBT topics in school.

What Feds Think is Important?

The settlement is significant in the context of workplace bullying because it sheds light on what steps the DOJ and the OCR deem to be important to address bullying and harassment. Also, the federal lawsuit relied upon laws that potentially could apply to any target of workplace bullying. In addition to Title IX, the federal lawsuit alleged violation of the Equal Protection Clause of the Fourteenth Amendment to the U.S. Constitution and Title IV of the Civil Rights Act of 1964, 42 U.S.C. §§ 2000c–2000c-9 (Title IV). Finally, the Minnesota settlement is more evidence of society's growing intolerance for bullying and harassment. If such harassment is no longer acceptable in schools, then why should it be acceptable in the workplace?

Among other things, the Minnesota settlement requires the District to:

– Retain an Equity Consultant to recommend any revisions to district policies related to harassment, as well as district procedures relating to the investigation and response to incidents of harassment, parental notification, and tracking of harassment incidents.

– Hire a Title IX/Equity Coordinator to implement district policies and procedures and monitor complaints to ensure that district administrators and staff adhere to sex and sexual orientation-based discrimination laws and to identify trends and common areas of concern.

- Develop better trainings on harassment for all students and employees who interact with students.
- Ensure that a counselor or other qualified mental health professional is available during school hours for students in need.
- Strengthen the District's annual anti-bullying survey.
- Work with the Equity Consultant to identify hot spots in district schools where harassment is problematic, including outdoor locations and school buses.
- Require District personnel to investigate, address, and respond appropriately to every harassment incident, whether reported (verbally or in writing) by the harassed student, a witness, a parent, or any other individual.
- Provide contact information, including the physical address, phone number and email address, for the District's Title IX Coordinator and Equity Coordinator.
- Develop procedures for parental notifications that are sensitive to privacy rights relating to a student's real or perceived orientation or gender identity.
- Provide a link on the school web site to an incident reporting form and allow direct electronic submission of complaints.

Harassment was defined in the federal lawsuit as "the use of derogatory language, intimidation, and threats; unwanted physical contact and/or physical violence, or the use of derogatory language and images in graffiti, pictures or drawings, notes, e-mails, electronic postings and/or phone messages related to a person's membership in a protected class."

The Minnesota settlement also ended a lawsuit filed by The Southern Poverty Law Center and the National Center for Lesbian Rights on behalf of the six complaining students, who received $270,000 in damages under the settlement.

Response to Complaint is Key

A key issue in student bullying cases under Title IX appears to be how the educational institution responded to complaints.

A federal judge in 2010 set aside a Michigan jury verdict that awarded $800,000 to Dane Patterson, 19, who filed a Title IX case against the Hudson Area School district after years of bullying and abuse in middle school and high school. The jury said Patterson was able to establish that he was subjected to severe harassment that the school district knew about and responded to with indifference.

Judge Lawrence P. Zatkoff, however, said the school district promptly investigated every one of Patterson's complaint of which it had notice. Therefore, Judge Zatkoff ruled, the school district was not completely indifferent because its actions were not unreasonable. The judge also said the harassment Patterson suffered was due to his unpopularity because of his scholarly and bookish nature and not sexual harassment. (See *Patterson v. Hudson Area Schools,* 724 F.Supp.2d 682 (2010)).

Patterson, who was routinely called "queer" and "faggot," filed the lawsuit after a fellow student stripped naked, forced Patterson into a corner, jumped on Patterson's shoulders, and rubbed his penis and scrotum on Patterson's neck and face. The student who sexually assaulted Patterson was prosecuted criminally and was formally expelled from the school.

Don't Forget Civil Rights Laws

The Office for Civil Rights (OCR) of the U.S. Department of Education issued a written guidance on Oct. 26, 2010 applauding nationwide efforts by school districts to adopt anti-bullying policies. The guidance states that "bullying fosters a climate of fear and disrespect that can seriously impair the physical and psychological health of its victims and create conditions that negatively affect learning, thereby undermining the ability of students to achieve their full potential." The OCR, however, reminded school systems that school bullying may trigger responsibilities under one or more of the federal anti-discrimination laws enforced by the OCR, including Title IX. The OCR said school districts that adopt anti-bullying policies may violate civil rights statutes "when peer harassment based on race, color, national origin, sex, or disability is sufficiently serious that it creates a hostile environment and such harassment is encouraged, tolerated, not adequately addressed, or ignored by school employees."

In addition to Title IX, the OCR enforces Title VII of the Civil Rights Act of 1964 (Title VII), which prohibits discrimination on the basis of race, color, or national origin; Section 504 of the Rehabilitation Act of 1973 (Section 504); and Title II of the Americans with Disabilities Act of 1990 (Title II). Section 504 and Title II prohibit discrimination on the basis of disability. Employee complaints that are filed with OCR are generally referred to the U.S. Equal Employment Opportunity Commission.

Title IX covers state education agencies, elementary and secondary school systems, colleges and universities, vocational schools, proprietary schools, state vocational rehabilitation agencies, libraries, and museums that receive U.S. Department of Education funds. Title IX does not cover educational institutions controlled by religious organizations if the act's application would be inconsistent "with the religious tenets of such organization;" military service organizations, social fraternities or sororities and the YMCA, YWCA, Girl Scouts and Boy Scouts, and other voluntary youth organizations that traditionally are limited to one sex and to persons less than 19 years of age.

A complaint can be filed by anyone who believes that an educational institution which receives federal financial assistance has discriminated against someone on the basis of race, color, national origin, sex, disability, or age. The person or organization filing the complaint need not be a victim of the alleged discrimination, but may complain on behalf of another person or group. The plaintiff may see seek punitive damages for intentional violations of the statute. Information about how to file a complaint with OCR can be found at

http://www2.ed.gov/about/offices/list/ocr/complaintintro.html

Summary: Title IX

Who is eligible: Title IX of the Education Amendments of 1972 protects people from discrimination based on sex in education programs or activities which receive federal financial assistance. Covered recipients include state and local governments, private entities, and individuals.

Major provisions: Title IX protects individuals from discrimination on the basis of sex by any program or activity receiving federal financial assistance. Title IX also affords a cause of action for retaliation.

Penalties: The U.S. Department of Education can impose administrative penalties and withdraw federal funding from an institution that violates Title IX. Individuals or groups may file a private cause of action seeking compensatory and punitive damages and attorney fees.

For more information, go to: go to: U.S. Department of Education Office of Civil Rights, at http://www2.ed.gov/about/offices/list/ocr/index.html?src=oc.

12. NATIONAL LABOR RELATIONS ACT

"If you want to go quickly go alone, if you want to go far go together." - African quote.

Not Just for Unions

The National Labor Relations Act (NLRA), 29 U.S.C. §§ 151-169, is generally associated with unions and union organizing. Most private sector employees don't know that the NLRA provides them with important protections from workplace abuse – and that's the way that employers want to keep it.

The National Labor Relations Board (NLRB) issued a rule that required most private sector employers to post a notice on November 14, 2011 advising employees of rights that workers have possessed for more than 70 years under the NLRA The NLRB said the notice was needed because "many employees protected by the NLRA are unaware of their rights under the statute." Requiring employers to post the notice would, according to the NLRB, "increase knowledge of the NLRA among employees, in order to better enable the exercise of rights under the statute."

There was an immediate outcry from business groups, including the U.S. Chamber of Commerce. They claimed the NLRB, an independent agency that resolves allegations of unfair labor practices, was interfering with the free market and hindering job creation. Several business groups sued the NLRB to stop the union poster rule, arguing the NLRB had exceeded its authority and violated the First Amendment by compelling employer speech. The NLRB delayed implementation of the rule until January 31, 2012 and then to April 30, 2012. Two weeks before the rule was to take effect the U.S. Court of Appeals for the District of Columbia issued a preliminary injunction to halt implementation of the rule, pending the outcome of an appeal.

In June 2013, the last stake may have been nailed in the coffin of the notice rule. The U.S. Court of Appeals for the Fourth Circuit in South Carolina ruled the NLRB lacks the authority to require employers to post notices either electronically or physically "in a conspicuous place" informing workers of their rights under the NLRA. The South Carolina court ruled the NLRB is not charged with informing employees of their rights under the NLRA and "we find no indication in the plain language of the Act that Congress intended to grant the Board the authority to promulgate such a requirement."

What They Don't Want You to Know

What employers don't want employees to know is that the NLRA affords most –even workers who have nothing to do with unions – the right to join together to improve their wages and working conditions. Section 7 of the NLRA guarantees employees the right to engage in "concerted activities" not only for self-organization but also "for the purpose of . . . mutual aid or protection. . . ." The broad protection of Section 7 applies with particular force to unorganized employees who, because they have no designated bargaining representative, must "speak for themselves as best they [can]." *NLRB v. Washington Aluminum Co.,* 370 U.S. 9, 14, 82 S. Ct. 1099, 8 L.Ed.2d 298 (1962).The NLRA can come into play, for example, when an employer fires a non-union employee or employees for discussing a safety concern or other concerns about working conditions.

In 2011, five non-union workers at a non-profit organization in Buffalo, N.Y. were fired for allegedly cyberbullying a co-worker. NLRB Administrative Law Judge Arthur J. Amchan later ruled the organization, Hispanics United of Buffalo, Inc. (HUB), wanted to downsize and "seized upon the Facebook posts as an excuse for doing so."

Lydia Cruz-Moore, a HUB employee, verbally accused co-workers on several occasions of slacking off. Then she threatened to complain to the program director. One of the co-workers involved initiated a Facebook discussion soliciting responses to Cruz-Moore's criticism. Five co-workers participated in the discussion. Some made sarcastic and derogatory comments about Cruz-Moore and HUB's clientele. When Cruz-Moore found out about the Facebook posts, she sent a text message to HUB's

Executive Director Lourdes Iglesias complaining that Cruz-Moore was the victim of cyberbullying. Iglesias fired the five employees for violating HUB's "zero-tolerance" harassment policy.

Judge Amchan discounted Iglesias' stated reasons for the terminations. He said the fired employees "were taking a first step towards taking group action to defend themselves against the accusations they could reasonably believe Cruz-Moore was going to make to management." Judge Amchan said the fact that the discussion occurred on Facebook was not a determining factor because HUB officials conceded the employees would have been fired even if their activity had taken place around the water cooler.

Judge Amchan said the Facebook discussion was protected under the NLRA because it involved the terms and conditions of employment – specifically, job performance and staffing levels. Amchan also noted the Facebook posts were not made at work nor during working hours, were not critical of HUB, and that HUB failed to prove the employees violated any specific policies or rules. He said it was irrelevant that persons other than HUB employees could see the Facebook postings.

By discharging all of the employees on the same day, Amchan said, "Respondent prevented them from taking any further group action vis-à-vis Cruz-Moore's criticisms." Moreover, Judge Amchan said, the fact that Iglesias fired the workers all at once "establishes that Respondent viewed the five as a group and that their activity was concerted." He concluded that the workers "Facebook communications with each other, in reaction to a co-worker's criticisms of the manner in which HUB employees performed their jobs, are protected."

Protected Concerted Activity

Generally, the right to engage in "protected concerted activity" under the NLRA is defined as when two or more employees take action for their mutual aid or protection regarding terms and conditions of employment. A single employee may engage in protected concerted activity if he or she is acting on the authority of other employees, bringing group complaints to the employer's attention, trying to induce group action, or seeking to prepare for group action.

A few examples of protected concerted activities are:

- Two or more employees address their employer about improving their pay.
- Two or more employees discuss work-related issues beyond pay, such as safety concerns, with each other.
- An employee speaks to an employer on behalf of one or more co-workers about improving workplace conditions.

The thing the NLRA does not protect is insubordination. Complaining about a supervisor generally is not protected because the selection and retention of a supervisor traditionally has been viewed as a management prerogative and not a matter of concern for subordinates. An employee who writes a blog that is read by the public and is critical of management soon may find himself or herself looking at a pink slip.

The NLRA is best known for protecting workers in the context of union organizing and activity. The NLRA forbids employers from interfering with, restraining, or coercing employees in the exercise of rights relating to organizing, forming, joining or assisting a labor organization for collective bargaining purposes, or from working together to improve terms and conditions of employment, or refraining from any such activity. Similarly, labor organizations may not restrain or coerce employees in the exercise of these rights.

The NLRA provides employees with the right to:

– Form, or attempt to form, a union;

– Join a union whether the union is recognized by the employer or not;

– Assist a union in organizing co-workers;

– Refuse to do any or all of the above.

Employer Bullying

Bullying is often reported by employees who demand a legal right, such as the right to overtime or equal pay. These workers often are labeled "troublemakers" and targeted for dismissal, especially in states that follow the employment at will rule.

Editors and reporters at the Santa Barbara News-Press in California were bullied by management when they tried to protect the integrity of news reporting in 2006. In one instance, a reporter and three editors were reprimanded for writing an article that included the future home address of actor Rob Lowe, who was a friend of one of the publishers. The NLRB later said this reprimand was an abrupt, unwarranted departure from the paper's longstanding practice of publishing the addresses of controversial building projects – as well as the name of the owner involved.

Another time, management issued a "gag order" to prevent employees from disseminating information about the paper to outside news outlets -- leading to the mass resignation of 15 editors and reporters. The publishers then discharged two reporters for "biased reporting," resulting in a public protest by the remaining employees. After that, the employees launched a union organizing effort and the animosities intensified.

In September 2011, the NLRB unanimously ruled that the News-Press publisher, Ampersand Publishing LLC, committed multiple unfair labor practices during the union organizing campaign. The NLRB said the publisher coercively interrogated employees concerning union activities, engaged in surveillance of union activities, required employees to lower the evaluation scores of union supporters, etc. The NLRB ordered the publisher to reinstate eight fired journalists. (See *Ampersand Publishing, LLC d/b/a Santa Barbara News-Press and Graphics Communications Conference International Brotherhood of Teamsters and Robert Guiliano*, 31-CA-027950 (NLRB, August 11, 2011)

Union Contract Clause

Many unions have negotiated a workplace anti-bully clause in their union contracts. For example, Massachusetts public employee unions affiliated with the Service Employees International Union (SEIU) and the National Association of Government Employees (NAGE) approved a new collective bargaining agreement in 2009 that protects more than 21,000 state workers from bullying and abusive supervision.

When a union and an employer agree to a collective bargaining agreement, both parties must abide by the provisions of the agreement. If the contract contains an anti-bully clause and the employer violates the clause, an employee has the right to file a grievance. If the grievance is denied, the union can file an unfair labor practice with the NLRB, which will investigate and issue a finding. A party that is aggrieved by a decision of the NLRB can seek review by petitioning in a federal court of appeals.

The NLRA also prohibits transferring, laying off, terminating, assigning employees more difficult work tasks, or otherwise punishing employees because they filed an unfair labor practice charge or participated in an investigation conducted by NLRB.

Summary: National Labor Relations Act

Who is eligible: Most private sector employees are covered under the NLRA; not covered are federal, state, or local government employees, agricultural laborers, home-based domestic workers, employees who are a parent or spouse, independent contractors, or employers subject to the Railway Labor Act (including railroads and airlines).

Major provisions: The NLRA regulates the relationship between labor and management. Employers cannot interfere with an employee's exercise of NLRA rights, including the right to right to join together to improve their wages and working conditions, *with or without* a union.

Penalties: Reinstatement, back wages, monetary fines, injunctive relief, attorney's fees.

For more information, go to the National Labor Relations Board at https://www.nlrb.gov/.

13. FAIR LABOR STANDARDS ACT

"Fairness is what justice really is."

> *- Supreme Court Justice Potter Stewart*

Rachel (not her real name) was required to attend a week-long out-of-state conference, where she was told to stand at a booth and hand out leaflets for 14 hours a day. When she asked if she would be paid overtime or compensatory time, she was told that she was not eligible because she was classified as an exempt employee under the Fair Labor Standards Act of 1938 (FLSA).

Two weeks later, her boss told Rachel on Friday afternoon that she had to work all weekend, typing up and making copies of a lengthy report. As a single mother, Rachel had difficulty finding last-minute childcare, which is a costly and unreimbursed expense.

"Can't you please find someone else? I have kids," she pleaded, near tears.

"If you don't work, don't bother showing up on Monday," replied her boss, shrugging.

To keep her job, Rachel did report to work that weekend but she also decided to speak to an attorney to find out her rights. She learned that her employer had misclassified her position as exempt under the Fair Labor Standards Act to avoid paying overtime. Despite her glorified title -- Resource Officer -- Rachel did secretarial and clerical work. She did not exercise discretion or independent judgment with respect to matters of significance, nor did she supervise anyone.

The Fair Labor Standards Act (FLSA), 29 U.S.C. 201, *et seq.,* addresses many of the abusive tactics that employers use to enrich themselves at the expense of their workers.

The FLSA sets the standards for basic minimum wage and overtime pay. It requires employers to pay covered employees who are not otherwise exempt at least the federal minimum wage. It requires overtime pay of one-and-one-half-times the regular rate after 40 hours in a workweek. The FLSA does not allow private sector workers to "donate" or "volunteer" work hours to their employers. It strictly prohibits working "off the clock."

Exempt Employees

Most public and private employees are covered by the FLSA but certain classes of employees are exempt. These include:

– Professional employees (lawyers, doctors, etc.)

– Managers who supervise at least two employees.

– Administrators whose primary job duty involves the exercise of discretion and independent judgment.

– Creative professionals or artists.

Courts and the U.S. Department of Labor (DOL), which administers the FLSA through its Employment Standards

Administration Wage and Hour Division, construe all of the exemptions narrowly. The burden of proof is on the employer.

One issue that has become more prominent in this era of smart phones involves employers that expect employees to monitor and respond to emails and text messages during their off-hours.

In *Allen v. City of Chicago*, 2011 WL 941383 (N.D. Ill. 2011), a federal judge refused to dismiss a class action lawsuit filed by Chicago Police Sergeant Jeffrey Allen, who said he was required to "routinely and regularly" respond to phone calls, e-mails and work orders off the clock. Allen said he was expected to answer his department issue BlackBerry throughout the night and into the early morning hours, even though he was off duty. He said the city failed to pay him or to keep records of his overtime.

The city countered that Allen received premium pay under his union contract to compensate him for overtime spent responding to messages, and that the amount of time involved was too minimal to qualify for FLSA compensation.

The Court was not persuaded and said that Allen's lawsuit was "plausible."

The FLSA also dictates how and when wages are to be paid to employees, and what deductions can be made. Wages generally are due on the regular payday for the pay period covered. Deductions from wages for such items as cash or merchandise shortages, employer-required uniforms, and tools of the trade, are illegal if they reduce the wages or overtime pay of employees below the minimum rate required by the FLSA. Employers also cannot charge employees for normal business expenses that should be the responsibility of the employer.

Working conditions for children also are covered by the FLSA. For nonagricultural operations, the FLSA restricts the hours that children under age 16 can work and forbids employing children under age 18 in hazardous jobs (i.e. coal mining, meat packing, logging, roofing, manufacturing fireworks, etc.). For agricultural operations, the FLSA prohibits employing children under age 16 by *non-family* employers during school hours and in hazardous jobs (i.e., operating large farm machinery, applying dangerous chemicals to crops, etc.).

Willful violators of the FLSA can be prosecuted criminally and fined up to $10,000. A second conviction may result in imprisonment. The DOL may bring suit for back pay and an equal amount in liquidated damages (double the amount of an award for lost or unpaid wages).The DOL also can obtain injunctions to restrain persons from violating the FLSA.

Retaliation

The FLSA contains an anti-retaliation clause that comes into play if a worker complains about a protected job condition and as a consequence suffers an adverse job action. An employer who discharges or otherwise discriminates against an employee who files an FLSA complaint is liable for legal and equitable relief, "including without limitation employment, reinstatement, promotion, and the payment of wages lost and an additional equal amount as liquidated damages." 29 U.S.C. §216(b)

Kevin Kasten claimed he was discharged in 2006 from his Wisconsin factory job because he verbally complained to company officials that the location of time clocks prevented workers from receiving credit for time they spent putting on and taking off work-related protective gear. A federal judge dismissed the case, ruling the FLSA's anti-retaliation provision did not cover "oral" complaints. The U.S. Supreme Court last year disagreed and reinstated Kasten's lawsuit. (See *Kasten v. Saint-Gobain Performance Plastic*, 131 S.Ct. 1325 (2011).

The U.S. Supreme Court said in a 6 to 2 opinion that the FLSA applies both to oral and written complaints. The Court explained that a narrow interpretation of the FLSA would undermine the Act's basic objective, which is to prohibit "labor conditions detrimental to the maintenance of the minimum standard of living necessary for health, efficiency, and general well-being of workers," 29 U. S. C. §202(a).

Companies that operate sweatshops are notorious for violating the FLSA. In *Lin v. Great Rose Fashion, Inc.*, No. 09–834 (E.D.N.Y). June 3, 2009), Chinese garment workers complained that they were deprived of a minimum wage and overtime pay and then were fired in retaliation for pursuing their rights to just compensation. A federal judge rejected as "patently false" the company's argument that the workers were independent contractors.

"The Plaintiffs were low-skilled, immigrant piece-workers toiling for long hours of manual labor in a garment factory... The Defendants' argument is nothing more than a transparent attempt to use a legal fiction to escape liability for their alleged labor abuses. The notion that these Plaintiffs acted as independent contractors outside the protection of the FLSA is so thoroughly without merit that it borders on an affront to the dignity of this court," wrote the judge.

The Court also said the factory owners retaliated against the plaintiffs by threatening them and intimidating them. A surveillance video showed an incident in which one of the owners, Ms. Xiao Yan Lin, berated one of the plaintiffs in front of other workers. Ms. Lin called the worker a "heartless person," cursed at her, and declared that she "was the one who had caused all this problem." Ms. Lin told the staff that anyone without legal immigration status would be eliminated because of the plaintiff's complaint. Co-workers subsequently turned on the worker, blaming her and repeating Ms. Lin's assertions. The worker's hours were cut and she was eventually fired. The Court states that the worker sought medical treatment from a psychiatrist as a result of these events and the financial strain of being unemployed. The Court denied a motion by the Defendants to dismiss the case on the grounds that they had closed down the factory. The issue of damages had not been resolved at this writing.

Summary: Fair Labor Standards Act

Who is Eligible: Most private and public employees are covered by the FLSA. Certain categories of employees are exempt. These categories include professionals such as lawyers and doctors; managers who supervise at least two employees; administrators whose primary job duty involves the exercise of discretion and independent judgment; creative professionals or artists.

Major Provisions: The FLSA establishes minimum wage, overtime pay, recordkeeping, and youth employment standards.

Penalties: Right to sue for back pay, damages up to equal amount of back pay, compensatory damages for retaliation, fines for repeated or willful violations, punitive damages for retaliation against claimants, imprisonment, attorney's fees and court costs. Violators can be barred from receiving government contracts, have goods seized, and lose business licenses.

For more information, go to U.S. Department of Labor Wage and Hour Division at http://www.dol.gov/whd/flsa/.

14. BULLYING AND HEALTH LAWS

"She's not happy unless everyone around her is panicked, nauseous or suicidal." - Andy Sachs in The Devil Wears Prada (2006)

Family and Medical Leave Act

Workplace bullying is a health issue. There is overwhelming research that workplace bullying causes stress and anxiety, loss of self-esteem, depression, apathy, irritability, memory disorders, sleep disorders and problems with digestion. Prolonged bullying is believed to cause increased incidences of depression and contribute to chronic disease, including cardiovascular disease. Studies have shown that targets often exhibit symptoms analogous to Post Traumatic Stress Disorder. Workplace bullying can potentially incapacitate a worker for years, and even lead to suicide.

The Family and Medical Leave Act of 1993 (FMLA), 29 U.S.C. § 2601 *et seq.*, offers targets the possibility of at least a temporary reprieve from the bullying. Workers who have used up all their sick leave and vacation time can turn to the FMLA if they can show they are suffering from "a serious health condition that makes the employee unable to perform the essential functions of his or her job." The essential functions of the job are the basic job duties that an employee must be able to perform, with or without reasonable accommodation.

The FMLA offers 12 workweeks of *unpaid* but job-protected leave in a 12-month period. Group health coverage is continued under the same terms and conditions as if the employee had not taken the leave. The employer must bring workers back to the same or an equivalent job – the same hours, duties, pay and working conditions.

The FMLA defines a "serious health condition" as "an illness, injury, impairment, or physical or mental condition that involves . . . [i]npatient care . . . Or [c]ontinuing treatment by a health care provider." See 29 C.F.R. §§ 825.114(a) (1), (2). A serious health condition generally involves any condition that causes at least three consecutive days of absence combined with two or more treatments by a health care provider. Anxiety and emotional distress may qualify as a serious health condition under the FMLA.

The FMLA covers public agencies, including state, local and federal employers, schools, and private-sector employers. The FMLA is regulated by the U.S. Department of Labor's Wage and Hour Division.

To be eligible for FMLA leave, an employee generally must have worked for an employer for at least 12 months, or at least 1,250 hours over the past 12 months. This 1,250 hour requirement can be satisfied in different ways, such as working

104 hours per month for 12 months or working 24 hours per week for 52 weeks. The employee also must have worked at a location where the company employs 50-or more-employees within a 75-mile radius.

An employee can take FMLA leave time in the same increment as the employee is paid -- for example, an hourly employee can take FMLA leave on an hourly basis. Twelve weeks of leave at 40 hours per week equals 480 hours a year. Workers who take FMLA leave go to the doctor, for example, can subtract the amount of FMLA time they took from their total allotment. The remaining time is what they have left in FMLA leave.

Common Defenses

Employers use these common defenses to an FMLA claim:
- The employee was not eligible because she (or her family member) did not actually have a serious health condition;
- The employee sought the leave in reaction to impending discipline;
- The employee had chronic attendance problems;
- The employee was a malingerer who used any excuse to avoid working.

The FMLA also protects workers from retaliation for exercising their right to FMLA leave. The FMLA says an employer may not "interfere with, restrain, or deny the exercise of or the attempt to exercise" an employee's FMLA rights. See 29 U.S.C. § 2615(a) (1). Generally, workers must show that they invoked their right to FMLA benefits, suffered an adverse employment decision, and the adverse decision was causally connected to their invocation of their FMLA rights. See, e.g., *Hayduk v. Johnstown*, 2010 WL 2650248 (3d Cir. July 2, 2010). An adverse employment decision includes demotion or dismissal.

A federal appeals court concluded in 2011 that a jury could find that William Shaffer, a supervisor at the American Medical Association, was the victim of retaliation because he requested six-weeks of FMLA leave so that he could undergo knee surgery. (*Shaffer v. American Medical Association*, 7th Cir., No. 10-2117 (Oct. 18, 2011)). Evidence in the case included an October 28, 2011 email exchange between AMA senior managers stating that one of Shaffer's subordinates was targeted for a lay off due to the economic downturn. Ten days after Shaffer made his request for FMLA leave on Nov. 10, 2010, the senior managers engaged in another email exchange in which they said Shaffer would be laid off, instead of his subordinate. Shaffer was laid off in December 2010.

Workers who request FMLA leave should do so in writing. A written or email request serves as evidence that the employer had notice of the FMLA leave request. This becomes important if the employer retaliates against the employee. Employers are not liable for retaliation unless they knew about the request for FMLA leave. If an employee made the request verbally, an unscrupulous employer can deny the request was made and argue that it could not therefore have considered the FMLA request when it demoted or fired the employee.

Bundling Claims

The FMLA is not a solution to workplace bullying, but it can be part of a solution. Attorneys for Plaintiffs often bundle an FMLA claim with other claims because the FMLA does not permit damages for emotional distress. For example, the FMLA was successfully paired with a state law claim of Intentional Infliction of Emotional Distress (IIED) in a 2002 case that involved workplace bullying. The plaintiff, Chris Schultz, Illinois hospital maintenance, won a jury award of almost $12 million. (*Schultz v. Advocate Health & Hospitals Corp.*, No. 01 C 0702 (N.D. Ill. 2002)).

Schultz, a 25-year veteran employee of Advocate Health and Hospital Corp.'s Christ Hospital and Medical Center in Oak Lawn, IL, requested FMLA leave to care for his dying parents. When he returned from FMLA leave after the death of his mother, he was fired because he failed to meet productivity goals established while he was on FMLA leave.

Schultz said his termination was part of a campaign of harassment by his manager, who was described as a bully by several witnesses at the trial. Prior to Shultz' FMLA leave, the manager persuaded a friend to goad Schultz into an argument, for which only Schultz was reprimanded. Schultz successfully challenged the reprimand and it was removed from his record.

Nonetheless, Schultz was transferred from his maintenance position on the main floor to the garbage pit in the hospital's morgue – to a job that previously was done by two employees. Then Schultz received his first poor performance review in 24 years. At this point, hospital staff nominated Schultz for the hospital's prestigious "MVP" award and Schultz won the honor.

Schultz said the impact of the harassment was heightened by the stress of caring for his parents which led to his application for FMLA leave.

Schultz's attorney, Charles Siedlecki of Chicago, argued that an employee who requests FMLA leave already is under stress and the application for FMLA leave "puts the employer on notice that the person seeking leave is particularly susceptible to emotional distress." The attorney cited a 2001 federal court decision holding that "behavior that otherwise might be considered merely rude, abrasive, or inconsiderate may be deemed outrageous if the defendant knows that the plaintiff is particularly susceptible to emotional turmoil." (See *Honaker v. Smith*, 256 F.3d 477 (7th Cir. 2001))

If Schultz had just filed an FMLA claim, the jury would have been severely limited in the amount of damages it could award him. Potential damages for an FMLA violation include reinstatement, front and back pay, and liquidated damages (doubling the total amount of compensation awarded). Adding the state law IIED claim allowed the jury to award Schultz $10 million in punitive damages, on top of $750,000 in compensatory damages. Schultz also was awarded $900,000 in damages from his two former supervisors.

An employer may ask an employee seeking FMLA leave to provide medical certification from a health care provider to verify the employee's serious health condition. *See* 29 U.S.C. § 2613 and 29 C.F.R. § 825.305. If such medical certification is requested, it becomes a basic qualification for obtaining FMLA leave. If the employee fails to comply, any leave taken is not considered FMLA-protected leave. *See* 29 C.F.R. § 825.312(b).

If the employer doubts the validity of the medical certification provided by the employee's medical provider, then the employer can, at its own expense, require the employee to obtain a second opinion. If the second opinion conflicts with the first opinion, the employer can request a third opinion, again at its own expense. *See* 29 C.F.R. § 825.307.

A civil complaint for a violation of the FMLA must be filed within two years of the "last event constituting the alleged violation" -- within three years if the violation is willful. *See* 29 U.S.C. § 2617(c) (1)-(2). A violation is willful if the employer either knew or displayed reckless disregard for whether the employer's conduct was prohibited by the law.

Summary: Family and Medical Leave Act

Who is eligible? An employee who has worked for a covered employer for a total of 12 months or 1,250 or more hours during the previous 12 months.

Major provisions: Up to 12 weeks of unpaid but job-protected leave in a 12-month period for a "serious health condition" of the employee or a family member.

Penalties: Back pay; reinstatement or front pay if reinstatement is not available; benefits; liquidated damages (double damages); attorneys' fees.

For more information, go to the U.S. Department of Labor's Wage and Hour Division at

http://www.dol.gov/whd/fmla/index.htm

Workers' Compensation

Workers' compensation is sometimes referred to as "the grand bargain" between employees and employers. At one time, verdicts were routinely reduced as a result of legal theories involving the negligence of the employee or his or her assumption of risk. For example, an employee could sue for injuries incurred if she fell on a broken stair at her workplace. The employer, however, could countersue for contributory negligence if, for example, the employee's shoelaces were untied and this might have contributed to the accident. In that way, the employer could reduce the amount of the worker's award.

But now the federal government - and every state - has a workers' compensation scheme that generally requires employees to be compensated without regard to fault for economic loss associated with employment-related injuries, illnesses, and deaths. In exchange for this guarantee, workers surrender their right to sue their employers for damages related to work-related injuries, illnesses, or deaths.

Workers' compensation laws may impact workplace bullying in two important ways:

- To the extent a mental or psychological problem arises out of working in an abusive environment in the course of employment, it may qualify as a workers' compensation claim under state law.

- Workers' compensation laws often preclude other avenues of legal redress on the basis that workers' compensation is considered the exclusive remedy for employment-related injuries.

There is much debate nationally about whether workers' compensation adequately compensates workers who are seriously injured on the job -- especially when they are injured as a result of the employer's gross negligence. This is especially true if an unscrupulous employer decides it is cheaper to pay injured workers under a state workers' compensation scheme than to correct conditions that result in injuries.

Intentional?

Plaintiff attorneys often seek to escape the confines of the workers' compensation "exclusivity rule" so that their client can collect not only compensatory damages but also punitive damages. Some states permit this legal option if the employee can establish an intentional tort claim, or show that the employer intentionally created a dangerous condition that made the plaintiff's injuries likely to occur.

In the context of workplace bullying, plaintiffs have successfully argued that their employers had notice of the bullying but failed to act, resulting in injuries.

A federal judge in West Virginia held in 2011 allowed a grocery store stocker who was injured on the job to seek damages in excess of the benefits available under the state's workers' compensation law because the employer had acted with "deliberate intention." (See *Skaggs v. Kroger Co.* No. 2:10-0768 (S.D.W. Va. 4/21/11))

The employee was injured when a malfunctioning pallet jack that ran over the worker's foot. The employer argued that it had no actual knowledge of the unsafe working condition and related risks. The Court, however, pointed to testimony that the faulty pallet jack led to another employee's hand injury and to plaintiff's statements to superiors that he was untrained in the use of the pallet jack.

Courts, however, are generally are reluctant to make exceptions to workers' compensation statutes.

In 2003, the U.S. Court of Appeals for the Ninth Circuit upheld the termination of a commissioner for a municipal court who claimed, among other things, that she was fired because she refused to fix tickets for the presiding judge's friends. (See *Bracke v. County of L.A.,* 60 Fed. Appx. 120, 2003 U.S. App. LEXIS 4204 (9th Cir. 2003). The appellate court said the plaintiff could not sue for either negligent or intentional infliction of emotional distress because the California's Workers' Compensation Act provides the exclusive remedy for injuries caused by fellow employees.

Similarly, the U.S. Court of Appeals for the Eighth Circuit in 2010 said that a Minnesota worker injured by a co-worker was barred by the state's workers' compensation law from bringing common law personal injury claims against her employer, including intentional infliction of emotional distress. (See *Fu v. Owens*, No. 09-2489 (8th Cir. 10/6/10). The case involved an assault against a nurse practitioner by her much taller, heavier assistant who had a prior criminal record. The appeals court said evidence of "specific, work-related" disputes between the two workers meant that the assault was covered by workers compensation because it occurred at work and was "inseparable" from the working conditions of the two employees.

Check with your state to determine the specific provisions of your state's worker's compensation law.

Americans with Disability Act

Targets of workplace bullying could assert that the impact of workplace bullying and abuse resulted in a disability for which they should receive a reasonable accommodation so they can continue working. A reasonable accommodation might be permission to use unpaid medical leave might, a modified work schedule or reassignment to another vacant position (away from

213

the supervision of a bully boss). A qualified disability can include depression, sleeplessness and other physical or emotional damage.

The Americans with Disabilities Act of 1990, (Pub. L. 101-336) (ADA) prohibits public entities, including state or local governments, from discriminating against individuals due to disability. According to the ADA: "[N]o qualified individual with a disability shall, by reason of such disability, be excluded from participation in or be denied the benefits of the services, programs, or activities of a public entity, or be subjected to discrimination by any such entity." The term "public entity" means any department, agency, special purpose district, or other instrumentality of a state or local government.

The federal government is subject to the Rehabilitation Act of 1973, 29 U.S.C. § 701-7961 (2006), which incorporates the ADA's substantive standards. 29 U.S.C. § 794(d); 29 C.F.R. § 1614.203(b) (2008).

The ADA defines "disability" as:

– A physical or mental impairment that substantially limits one or more of the major life activities of [an] individual;

– A record of such impairment;

– Being regarded as having such impairment.

The ADA and the Rehabilitation Act generally do not protect an employee who cannot perform the essential functions of the job even with an accommodation. They protect the employee who, with reasonable accommodations, can do the job in spite of a disability. Also, an employer can assert that it is unable to accommodate the employee because to do so would pose an unreasonable hardship. For example, an employer does not have to create a "light duty" position if none exists.

Mental Impairment

The U.S. Equal Employment Opportunity Commission (EEOC) says a mental impairment under the Americans with Disabilities Act is "[a]ny mental or psychological disorder, such as . . . emotional or mental illness." Examples given by the EEOC include major depression, bipolar disorder, anxiety disorders (which include panic disorder, obsessive compulsive disorder, and Post Traumatic Stress Disorder.

Impairment under the ADA must substantially limit one or more major life activities to rise to the level of a "disability." A life activity may include learning, thinking, concentrating, interacting with others, caring for oneself, speaking, performing manual tasks, sleeping or working. Whether a disability substantially limits a life activity depends upon the individual's typical level of functioning at home, at work, and in other settings, as well as evidence showing that the individual's functional limitations are linked to his/her impairment.

Some factors considered by courts to determine whether an individual is *substantially* limited in a major life activity are:

– The nature and severity of the impairment;

– The duration or expected duration of the impairment;

-The permanent or long term impact or the expected permanent or long term impact of the impairment.

The EEOC states that an employee who asks for time off because s/he is "depressed and stressed has put the employer on notice that s/he is requesting accommodation. The employer may require reasonable documentation that the employee has a disability within the meaning of the ADA and, if s/he has such a disability, that the functional limitations of the disability necessitate time off. The employer may ask the employee to sign a limited release allowing the employer to submit a list of specific questions to the employee's health care professional about his or her condition and need for reasonable accommodation.

Targets of workplace bullying commonly experience stress and anxiety. The severity of the harm they suffer is influenced by the intensity and duration of the bullying. Research by a leading British psychologist, Dr. Noreen Tehrani, suggests that severely bullied workers experience post-traumatic stress (which is a covered disability under the ADA). Dr. Tehrani said these workers experience hyper arousal, a feeling of constant anxiety and over-vigilance; avoidance of anything to do with the traumatizing event; and re-experiencing, in which subjects suffer flashbacks or obsessive thoughts concerning the trauma. Dr. Tehrani said bullied workers may go through the same emotions and stresses as battle-scarred troopers. "The symptoms displayed by people who have been in conflict situations and workplaces where bullying happens are strikingly similar," she said.

Employers covered by the ADA must insure that workers with disabilities have an equal opportunity to apply for jobs, to work and be promoted in jobs for which they are qualified. Workers with disabilities have a right to equal access to the same benefits and privileges that are offered to other employees, including health insurance or training. Finally, the ADA requires employers to insure that persons with a disability are not harassed. In some federal circuits, it is a per se violation of the ADA to base a disciplinary decision on conduct resulting from a disability.

Stress Part of Job?

There are potential drawbacks to using the ADA for workplace bullying claims. Courts tend to view abuse and stress as being intrinsic to employment, and often interpret workplace bullying to be a type of interpersonal conflict that is not covered under the ADA.

Susan Stefan, a noted expert in mental disability law, says many plaintiffs lose their ADA lawsuits because: "While courts understand that accessible workplaces may require teletypewriters or ramps, and that neither sexual harassment nor race discrimination is an employer prerogative, stress, punishing hours, overwork, unpleasant personality conflicts, and even worker abuse are much more commonly seen as simply intrinsic features of the workplace." (See, Susan Stefan, *"You'd Have to Be Crazy to Work Here": Worker Stress, The Abusive Workplace, and Title I of the ADA*, 31 Loyola Los Angeles Law Review, 795, (1998))

Stefan studied thousands of court cases involving the ADA and psychiatric disability. She said most of these cases involved abusive or stressful work environments with very long hours and bullying supervisors. Stefan said in most cases the workplace environment could have easily been remedied by the employer but was not. For example, she said, employers refused to reassign individuals who complained of bullying or to reduce the hours of workers who were working double shifts.

Instead of protecting vulnerable workers, Stefan says, courts shield abusive employers from the consequences of their actions. "Courts' generalizations that the ability to cope with virtually any level of stress is essential to maintaining employment in this country often insulate levels of abuse or extreme working conditions unnecessary to any job's function," she writes.

Summary: Americans with Disabilities Act

Who is eligible? Generally, employers who have had 15 or more employees for each working day in each of the 20 or more calendar weeks in the current or preceding year. Exempt are the U.S. government, Indian tribes, and bona-fide private clubs.

Major provisions: Prohibits public entities from discriminating against a person who has a physical or mental impairment that substantially limits one or more major life activities (like sitting, standing, sleeping or working).

Penalties: Compensatory and punitive damages.

For more information, go to
http://www.eeoc.gov/laws/statutes/ada.cfm

OSHA

As noted previously, workers who are bullied suffer a range of potentially serious short-term and long term health impacts, from anxiety to chronic disease. The U.S. Congress passed the Occupational Safety and Health Act of 1970 to assure safe and healthful working conditions for employees. Yet the federal government essentially has ignored workplace bullying as a workplace health and safety issue.

The Occupational Safety and Health Administration (OSHA), a division of the U.S. Department of Labor, was created by the OSH Act "…to assure so far as possible every working man and woman in the nation safe and healthful working conditions and to preserve our human resources." OSHA has issued standards for a wide variety of workplace industrial hazards, including toxic substances, fire and explosion hazards, machine hazards and infectious diseases. But OSHA has not issued standards with respect to workplace bullying –even though many other industrialized countries have such laws, and, despite a growing body of evidence that bullying causes targets to suffer potentially severe mental and physical harm.

When no specific OSHA standards exist, employers must comply with the OSH Act's "general duty clause." This clause,

Section 5(a)(1), requires that each employer "furnish ... a place of employment which is free from recognized hazards that are causing or are likely to cause death or serious physical harm to employees."

The OSH Act gives employees and/or their representatives the right to file a complaint if they believe there is a serious hazard. Furthermore, the Act gives complainants the right to request that their names not be revealed to their employers and the right to be protected from retaliation. Targets of workplace bullying may wish to exercise their right to complain to OSHA, if only to insure that OSHA is aware of the problem of workplace bullying in the United State

Summary: Occupational Safety and Health Act

Who is eligible: Most private-sector and federal employees. Coverage is provided directly by federal OSHA or through an OSHA-approved state program. The Act excludes self-employed, family farm workers, and state/local government workers (except in states that operate their own OSH plan).

Major provisions: The OSH Act protects employees from recognized hazards in the workplace, including exposure to toxic chemicals, excessive noise, mechanical dangers, heat or cold stress, or unsanitary conditions.

Penalties: Any employer who willfully or repeatedly violates the Act or regulations prescribed pursuant to this Act, may be assessed a civil penalty of not more than $70,000 for each violation, but not less than $5,000 for each willful violation. If a death occurs as a result of the willful violation, the employer could be subject to imprisonment.

15. WRONGFUL TERMINATION

"Hope has two beautiful daughters: their names are anger and courage. Anger that things are the way they are. Courage to make them the way they ought to be."
- St. Augustine

Contract for Service

Employment agreements are contracts of service.

The legal definition of a contract is "a promise or set of promises for the breach of which the law gives a remedy, or the performance of which the law in some way recognizes as a duty."

It is implied in contract law that the parties to a contract will act in good faith to perform and enforce the contract. This means that the parties will deal with each other honestly and fairly, so as to not destroy the right of the other party to receive the benefits of the contract. Each party has a duty to refrain from doing anything that would render performance of the contract impossible -- and also the duty to do everything that the contract presupposes that each party will do to accomplish its purpose. Failure to perform these duties results in a breach of the contract.

So how is it that employers are able to arbitrarily alter conditions of employment – change an employee's job description, require employees to work double overtime, and subject workers to abusive managers who make it impossible to perform for them to perform their job and receive the benefit of the contract?

Judge Wood's Rule

The answer is that employment contracts are treated differently from other types of contracts. The precedent for this distinction is an obscure 1877 treatise by Massachusetts Judge Horace Gray Wood. In A *Treatise on the Law of Master and Servant,* Judge Wood wrote:

"With us the rule is inflexible, that a general or indefinite hiring is *prima facie* a hiring at will, and if the servant seeks to make it out a yearly hiring, the burden is upon him to establish it by proof . . . . [I]t is an indefinite hiring and is determinable at the will of either party, and in this respect there is no distinction between domestic and other servants."

Judge Wood cited a mere four cases to support his proposition that workers can be fired without good cause.

Prior to Wood's rule, American courts followed the English common law rule holding that an employment contract for an indefinite period was extended for one year unless there was reasonable cause to discharge.

Despite its flimsy foundation, the "Wood's rule" was adopted by the New York Court of Appeals in 1895 in *Martin v. New York Life Insurance Co.*, 42 N.E. 416, 417 (N.Y. 1895)) and was thereafter routinely cited as the "employment-at-will" rule. It quickly spread to other states and became the *de facto* law of the land. It remains so today in every state except Montana, which carved out an exception that requires public employers to have just cause to fire public employees.

The employment-at-will rule essentially eliminates the requirement that both parties act in good faith. It holds that the employment contract is terminable at any time, by either party, with or without cause, absent an express agreement to the contrary. An employer can fire an employee for any reason – even a morally repugnant reason – so long as the employer does not violate a law (ex. race or sex discrimination) or an important public policy. Furthermore, the burden is on the discharged employee to show that the parties agreed to limit the employer's right to terminate the employee at will.

The original purpose of the "at will" doctrine was to afford employees the freedom to enter into contracts to suit their needs and to allow employers to exercise their best judgment with regard to employment matters. Some legal experts now argue that the doctrine serves primarily to give employers legal cover to dismiss good employees without cause.

When a worker is bullied on the job, and the employer does not protect the worker, the employer has failed to provide the worker with the safe and reasonable working conditions that are an implied part of the employment contract. The employer's breach of contract is particularly egregious when the bully is the boss.

Impossible to Perform

A bully boss systematically erects impediments to the target's success. Targets may be given unrealistic deadlines or receive incomplete instructions. They may be isolated or subjected to public humiliation and verbal abuse. Even if targets do excellent work, the bully may fault their performance in job ratings and evaluations. Eventually, many targets become psychologically incapable of delivering optimal performance as a result of fear and self-doubt caused by bullying.

One of the most appalling aspects of workplace bullying is that it is used strategically by employers to drive out good and hard-working employees. Employers might use bullying to downsize without paying unemployment benefits or to avoid a legal duty, such as paying workers' compensation. Such strategic harassment is a deliberate breach of the employment contract.

If the contract in question was for paving a driveway or for the sale of a cord of wood -- instead of employment services – judges would readily see that the employer's breach made it impossible for the target to perform. But thanks to that 1877 ruling seemingly pulled out of thin air by an obscure Massachusetts judge, most courts do not view employment as a contractual issue unless there is a specific contract.

The United States is the only major industrial power that maintains a general employment-at-will rule. Canada, France, Germany, Great Britain, Italy, Japan, and Sweden all have adopted laws requiring employers to show good cause for discharging employees. It is estimated that 70 million American workers are subject to the employment-at-will rule, including 15 percent of union workers and public employees.

Express and Implied Contracts

An express – or written – employment contract obviously offers employees greater protection from wrongful termination than is available to "at will" employees. Written contracts generally include a specific period of employment, and prevent the employer from terminating the employee during the employment period without "good cause." The contract also may specify what acts constitute good cause.

If an employment contract states that employees will only be fired "for cause," the burden is on the employer to document a valid cause. There are, of course, myriad reasons that an employee can be terminated for good cause, including poor performance, stealing, lying, failing a drug or alcohol test, falsifying records, embezzlement, insubordination, deliberating violating company policy or rules, and other serious misconduct.

Not all employment contracts are in written form. A contract can be implied from the circumstances of employment or from documents created by the employer, such as a written offer of employment or a policy manual that outlines the company's discipline or termination protocols. And an oral contract can be created by verbal guarantees made to the employee by the employer. (i.e., "You have a job here as long as you want one.")

To pursue a wrongful termination action for breach of an implied or oral contract, the employee must show the employer violated a tenet of the contract. For example, if the policy manual guarantees that an employee is entitled to three warnings prior to termination and an employee is fired after receiving only one warning, there may be grounds to file a wrongful termination action.

In *Toussaint v. Blue Cross and Blue Shield of Michigan*, 292 N.W.2d 880 (Mich. 1980), the Michigan Supreme Court became the first in the country to rule that an employer creates an "obligation" when it indicates that it has employment policies and practices in place that are fair and uniformly applied to each employee.

In 1967, Charles Toussaint interviewed for a job as a financial officer with Blue Cross/Blue Shield of Michigan. During the interview process, he was told that "as long as I did my job," he would be employed until retirement, and that "if I came to Blue Cross, I wouldn't have to look for another job because [the interviewer] knew of no one ever being discharged." He also was given a 260-page employee manual in which the company declared that its policy was to fire only for "just cause." Toussaint was subsequently fired. He filed a lawsuit for breach of contract and a trial court jury awarded him $72,000 in damages.

The Massachusetts Supreme Court ruled that the interview statements and employee manual amounted to an "implied contract" that included just-cause termination. "The employer secures an orderly, cooperative and loyal work force in exchange for job security ... Having announced the policy, presumably with a view to obtaining the benefit of improved employee attitudes and behavior and improved quality of the work force, the employer may not treat its promise as illusory," concluded the Court.

The Employer's Escape Hatch

Employers often find ways to get around the rights "guaranteed" in implied and oral contracts.

Thirty-seven male dealers and floorwalkers at Hilton Hotel's Las Vegas casino were fired in 1983 as they came off their shifts. (See *Brooks v. Hilton Casinos Inc.*, 959 F.2d 757, 7 (1992)) They filed a lawsuit alleging, among other things, breach of contract and bad faith discharge. They said a provision in Hilton's employee handbook setting forth a progressive discipline system was not followed. Also, some of the workers said they were verbally assured by Hilton management that they would continue to be employed as long as they did their jobs properly.

In a 9-3 decision, the U.S. Court of Appeals for the 9th Circuit ruled that the progressive discipline scheme outlined in the Hilton employee handbook was not controlling because it did not explicitly modify Hilton's right to fire at-will. The Court said the assurances of continued employment were "stray remarks" that were insufficient to defeat the employment-at-will rule.

Note: Hilton was found liable under another legal theory – The pool of new employees hired by Hilton to replace the fired dealers included 24 females and 13 males; the Court said the disproportionate number of new female hires supported the claim that the male dealers' were victims of sex discrimination.

The Hilton casino workers case shows that implied promises to workers easily can be rendered meaningless by the employer. For example, the employer may include a disclaimer in the employee handbook that *prevents* other language in the handbook (such as the promise of a progressive discipline system) from negating the employment-at-will rule. An example of such a disclaimer is:

> "While the Company may elect to follow its progressive discipline procedure, the Company is in no way obligated to do so. Using progressive discipline is at the sole discretion of the company in an employment-at-will workplace."

Such a disclaimer may not hold up, however, if the wording is not clear, the disclaimer is not prominent enough, the disclaimer is inconsistent with another policy statement, or the disclaimer is not adequately communicated to the employee.

Penalty for Breach of Contract

The remedy for breach of contract is:

- *Contractual Damages*. These are monetary damages that put the employee in as good a position as if the employer had fully performed the contract.

- *Loss of Benefit of Contract*. This may include lost wages, lost raises and bonuses, lost employee benefits (i.e. profit sharing, retirement benefits, and stock options). The employee also may be entitled to past monetary damages and future monetary damages.

- *Consequential losses*. The target can recover for harms arising as a consequence of the wrongful termination if such harm was within foreseeable to the parties at the time of making the contractual agreement.

* **Note:** Punitive damages generally are not available in contract actions, but if the conduct that causes the breach also constitutes a tort or personal injury, punitive damages may be available.

Exceptions to Employment-at-Will

Most U.S. workers are "at will" employees and if they are bullied they are vulnerable to unfair termination. Since the 1950s, however, most states have smoothed out some of the rough edges of the "at will" employment doctrine by creating statutory exceptions. Targets of workplace abuse should look to their state law to determine whether any exception to the "at will" rule would apply to their circumstances.

Exceptions to the employment-at-will doctrine generally serve to rebut or void the application of the doctrine, essentially requiring the employer to show that it had just cause to fire an employee. If an employer violates an exception to the doctrine, the terminated employee can bring an action for wrongful discharge. Common exceptions to the employment-at-will doctrine include:

- A written employment contract includes a fixed term of employment and no countervailing "at will" provision;
- An oral or "implied" contract obligates the employer to have *just cause* to terminate the employee (i.e. provision in employee handbook.)
- A discharge is conducted in a manner that violates a collective bargaining agreement. (Targets generally seek redress through their union, which may file a grievance.)
- A state or federal statute exists that protects the employee, such as an anti- discrimination law. (i.e., Title VII of the Civil Rights Act of 1964 and its state-law equivalents, the Age Discrimination in Employment Act, the Pregnancy Discrimination Act, the Worker Adjustment and Retraining Notification Act or WARN Act, and the Americans with Disabilities Act.)
- The employer cannot fire an employee if doing so violates an important public policy, such as firing an employee because he or she refused to do something illegal.

About a dozen states also recognize a general exception to the employment-at-will doctrine called an "implied covenant of good faith and fair dealing." This covenant is adapted from contract law: "Every contract imposes upon each party a duty of good faith and fair dealing in its performance and its enforcement." (See *Restatement (Second) of Contracts* §205). The term "good faith" is defined in the Uniform Commercial Code § 1-201(19) as "honesty in fact in the conduct or transaction concerned." The covenant of good faith and fair dealing may apply if the employer uses bad faith by, for example, firing an employee to avoid a legal duty (i.e., paying workers' compensation).

Public Policy Exception

Targets of workplace bullying who are neither union members nor members of a protected class under federal or state discrimination laws might still be able to show wrongful discharge in violation of "public policy" (i.e. whistleblowing; reporting for jury duty; refusing to do something illegal; requesting a legally recognized right).

Typically, public policy exceptions to the at-will rule are triggered when an employee is terminated in a manner that offends a public policy set forth in a court decision or state statutes. For example, the public policy exception is often invoked when an employer fires an employee who reported illegal company activity to law enforcement or regulatory authorities. Courts reason that permitting an employer to fire a whistleblower would undermine the important public policy of protecting the health and safety of the public.

To qualify for whistleblower protection, the employee's complaint generally must involve a serious infraction of a well-established and specific regulation or law pertaining to a recognized public policy. It cannot be a generalized complaint involving a vague law.

In *Margiotta v. Christian Hospital Northeast Northwest d/b/a Christian Hospital and BJC Health System*, No. SC90249 (Mo. 2/9/2010), the Missouri Supreme Court affirmed the dismissal of a case brought by an at-will employee who alleged he was terminated for reporting violations of federal and state regulations. The Court said the medical image technician, Daniel J. Margiotta, complained to his superiors about patient care, but cited a state regulation that dealt with building safety rather than patient treatment. The Court said that a "vague or general statute, regulation, or rule" cannot be the basis of an at-will wrongful termination theory, because it would force the court to decide on its own what the public policy requires. "The pertinent inquiry . . . is whether the authority clearly prohibits the conduct at issue in the action," said the Court.

Most states treat the so-called "public-policy" exception as a tort – an injury that does not involve a contract that results in damages. This concept was first recognized by the California Supreme Court in 1959. The remedy for a tort can be much higher than contractual damages, because it includes not only lost earnings but pain and suffering and punitive damages.

Jennifer Scott, a director at a private preschool in Rocklin, CA operated by Phoenix Schools Inc., was fired in 2006 when she refused to enroll a toddler on a day when no teachers were available to work in the classroom for two-year-olds. The parents complained to corporate headquarters and Scott was immediately terminated for "failing to maximize enrollment."

Scott, who had worked at the school for 12 years, was awarded $1.8 million in a wrongful termination and whistleblower retaliation lawsuit. The jurors said she was fired for refusing to violate California laws regarding student-teacher ratios. She was awarded $100,000 in lost past wages, $500,000 in lost future wages, $500,000 for emotional distress and $750,000 punitive damages. **Note**: An appeals court later overturned the punitive damages portion of the jury's award, finding there was insufficient evidence that Phoenix acted with malice. (See *Scott v. Phoenix Schools, Inc.,* 75 Cal.App.4th 702 (2009)).

In a case of alleged strategic harassment, DeWayne Sutton was fired on April 14, 2008, within an hour of informing the company president that he had injured his back while disassembling a chop saw as part of his job at Tomco Machining, Inc. He was given no reason for his dismissal. The company president said it was not because of Sutton's work ethic, job performance or because Sutton had violated company policy.

Sutton, who had worked at Tomco for more than two years, filed a lawsuit alleging Tomco violated an Ohio law that prohibits employers from retaliating against an employee for pursuing workers' compensation benefits. Sutton also filed a common-law tort claim for wrongful discharge in violation of public policy.

The trial court dismissed Sutton's complaint on the grounds that Ohio law only applied to injured workers who actually had filed a workers' compensation claim, not to those who merely expressed an intention to do so.

The Ohio Supreme Court, in a 4-3 decision (*Sutton v. Tomco Machining, Inc.*, 129 Ohio SC.3d 153 (2011)), reversed the lower court ruling, stating the Ohio General Assembly did not intend to leave a gap in protection that allowed employers to retaliate against employees who might pursue workers' compensation benefits.

Narrowly Interpreted

Although Sutton prevailed, many courts interpret the public policy exception to the "at will" rule so narrowly that it is difficult for even the most obviously deserving plaintiffs to prevail.

Karen Bammert was fired in 1997 from her job at Don's SuperValu, Inc. in Menomonie, Wisconsin, after her husband, a Menomonie police officer, assisted in the arrest of her employer's wife on a charge of drunk driving. Ms. Bammert filed a wrongful discharge lawsuit contending that it violated the public policy exception of the "at will" doctrine to fire her in retaliation for her husband's role in the arrest of her boss's wife. The Wisconsin Supreme Court agreed that the reason for Ms. Bammert's termination was "reprehensible," but said that it did not fall within the public-policy exception. "Of course, a natural sense of outrage over the facts alleged in this case brings on a desire to see the law provide a remedy, but it does not," the Court concluded. (See *Bammert v. Don's SuperValu, Inc.,* 646 NW 2d 365 (2002)

Constructive Discharge

Targets who feel they are being bullied may feel they have no choice but to quit to safeguard their emotional and physical well-being. Quitting, however, may result in denial of state unemployment compensation benefits and may have ramifications with respect to a potential lawsuit. If targets can show they left the job through no fault of their own – because they were effectively fired or laid off – they may be able to circumvent these problems.

The constructive discharge concept originated in the 1930s. The National Labor Relations Board (NLRB) developed the doctrine to address situations in which employers who had engaged in union activities were coerced into resigning, often by employers who created intolerable working conditions. The NLRB requires employees to establish two elements to prove a constructive discharge:

– The employer must impose burdens upon the employee that "cause, and [are] intended to cause, a change in his working conditions so difficult or unpleasant as to force him to resign."

- Secondly, the plaintiff must show those burdens were imposed because of the employee's union activities." (See *Crystal Princeton Refining Co.*, 222 N. L. R. B. 1068, 1069 (1976)).

Constructive discharge occurs when there is a unilateral breach by the employer of an express or implied term of the employment contract. Constructive discharge deals with a one-sided and fundamental change to the employment agreement that effectively results in an employee being wrongfully dismissed. What constitutes a fundamental change depends on the particular facts of the case – it generally must be a significant and not minor change. Abusive conduct on the part of the employer may be grounds for constructive dismissal. Courts, however, closely examine whether the plaintiff could have stayed on the job without fear of continuing abuse.

James McKelvey was an Army soldier who lost his right hand in 2004 while trying to defuse a roadside bomb. Two years later, after he had recovered from his wounds, McKelvey accepted a civilian job in the Army as an operations specialist, first at Selfridge Air National Guard Base and eventually at the Detroit Arsenal. McKelvey said that for nine months his supervisor and a co-worker repeatedly denigrated him with terms like "all fucked up," "a piece of shit," "worthless," and "a fucking cripple." McKelvey finally quit in 2007 and filed a lawsuit in which he claimed he was forced to quit – or constructively discharged – due to disability discrimination that resulted in a hostile work environment.

A Michigan federal court jury awarded McKelvey $4.4 million in damages on the constructive discharge claim. But the award was overturned by the trial judge as unsupported by law. The Army had argued that McKelvey could not support a claim of constructive discharge because management had intervened and McKelvey's working conditions improved two months *before* he quit. McKelvey appealed the trial court's ruling and the U.S. District Court of Appeals for the 6th Circuit ruled in 2011 that McKelvey *was* constructively discharged. But the appeals court did agree with the lower court that the proper remedy was job reinstatement – not the $4.4 million awarded by the jury. (See *McKelvey v. Secretary of United States Army,* No. 10-1172 (6th Cir. Dec. 14, 2011)).

Time to Leave?

Courts generally expect employees to remain on the job while pursuing relief from harassment. (See *Porter v. Erie Foods, Int'l,* 576 F.3d 629, 639–40 (7th Cir. 2009)). However, many targets of workplace bullying feel their working conditions are so intolerable that they must quit or face the prospect of serious mental or physical illness.

Constructive discharge sometimes offers targets who quit their jobs the possibility of retaining important legal rights under the law. Upon a successful showing of constructive discharge, plaintiffs are eligible for all of the damages they would be eligible for if they had been fired. For example, an employee who quits may forfeit the right to collect unemployment benefits, but an employee who is constructively discharged – which is considered the same as being fired – can collect unemployment benefits.

Given the lack of any state or federal law prohibiting workplace bullying, it may not be easy for targets to convince fact-finders that their workplace was so unbearable they were forced to quit. It is usually in the best interests of targets to consult with an attorney in their state prior to quitting to determine whether and how the theory of constructive discharge might apply in their case.

Constructive discharge is a form of wrongful termination. It introduces an important distinction with respect to an employer's potential liability in many different types of employment actions. It is the equivalent of an adverse job action and under federal civil rights laws eliminates certain defenses that would otherwise be available to an employer.

Claims that involve a "hostile environment" under civil rights laws often are coupled with claims of constructive discharge. The U.S. Equal Employment Opportunity Commission says most courts hold an employer liable for constructive discharge when the employer imposes intolerable working conditions in violation of Title VII, and when those conditions foreseeably would compel a reasonable employee to quit – regardless of whether the employer intended to force the victim's resignation. (See *i.e.*, *Derr v. Gulf*

Oil Corp., 796 F.2d 340, 343-44 (10th Cir. 1986); *Goss v. Exxon Office Systems Co.*, 747 F.2d 885, 888 (3d Cir. 1984)).

The U.S. Supreme Court said in *Pa. State Police v. Suders,* 542 U.S. 129, 147 (2004)), that a constructive discharge occurs when an employer essentially coerces an employee to leave by creating "working conditions so intolerable that a reasonable person in the employee's position would have felt compelled to resign." The Court said that Nancy Drew Suders, a police communications officer, suffered egregious sexual harassment, including "name calling, repeated episodes of explicit sexual gesturing, obscene and offensive sexual conversation and the posting of vulgar images."

Suders said that the station commander spoke to her about people having sex with animals, and a co-worker frequently grabbed his private parts and yelled obscenities involving oral sex. She told the department Equal Opportunity Officer that she was being harassed and was afraid. The officer, however, was not helpful. Instead, two days after complaining, Suders was arrested, handcuffed and photographed for the alleged theft of her own computer-skills exam papers. She had removed the papers after concluding that the supervisors falsely reported that she had repeatedly failed, when in fact, the exams were never forwarded for grading.

A district court judge dismissed Suders' constructive discharge case before it went to trial. The judge said Suders had failed to file a formal complaint pursuant to internal procedures set up by the state police to deal with sexual harassment. The trial court also said the police had not taken a "tangible employment action" (i.e., demotion or dismissal) that substantially changed her employment status.

Upon appeal, the Third Circuit Court of Appeals disagreed, ruling that the harassment was so bad that Suders had no choice but to quit. Because police were responsible for her resignation, the appeals court said, they could not use as a defense her failure to avail herself of remedial measures.

Employee Should Follow the Rules

The U.S. Supreme Court agreed to reinstate the case but disagreed with the Third Circuit Appeals Court's reasoning in one respect. The Supreme Court said an employee faced with a situation in which a "reasonable person... would have felt compelled to resign" can bring suit even if he or she had not filed a complaint with the employer before resigning. The employer, however, could use the employee's failure to file a complaint, along with evidence of the safeguards it had taken to prevent harassment, in its defense.

Using the Supreme Court's reasoning in *Suders*, an employer can potentially escape liability if it can prove the employee did not act to prevent the harassment, and the employer had safeguards in place would have prevented the harm if the employee had acted. The lesson is that targets should follow their employer's procedures (if any) with respect to reporting harassment.

When it's Reasonable to Leave

The Fifth Circuit Court of Appeals on September 12, 2011 recognized a constructive discharge claim in the context of the Age Discrimination in Employment Act.

In *Dediol v. Best Chevrolet Inc.*, No. 10-30-767 (5th Cir. 9/12/2011)), the 5th Circuit court said that Milan Dediol, a 65-year-old car salesman, could proceed to trial on his claim that he was forced to quit because age discrimination resulted in a hostile work environment.

Dediol said that his supervisor at the car dealership regularly referred to him as "old mother******," "old man," and "pops." He also said the supervisor physically intimidated him, threatening to 'kick [Dediol's] ass" and, at one time, the supervisor took off his shirt and said, "You don't know who you are talking to. See these scars. I was shot and was in jail." Dediol said he asked the General Manager for a transfer to the new car division, prompting the bullying supervisor to say: "Get your old f*****g ass over here. You are not going to work with new cars." Dediol said he finally quit after the supervisor physically charged him in front of nine to ten other workers, saying, "I am going to beat the 'F' out of you."

In its ruling, the Appeals Court said that to prove constructive discharge a party must show that "a reasonable party in his shoes would have felt compelled to resign." To determine if a reasonable employee would feel compelled to resign, the Court said the following factors are relevant:

– Demotion;

– Reduction in salary;

– Reduction in job responsibility;

– Reassignment to menial or degrading work;

– Reassignment to work under a younger supervisor;

–Badgering, harassment, or humiliation by the employer calculated to encourage the employee's resignation;

– Offers of early retirement or continued employment on terms less favorable than the employee's former status.

The Appeals Court concluded that Dediol had produced sufficient evidence to allow a jury to conclude that he was constructively discharged because he was the target of a hostile work environment on the basis of age, and that a reasonable person in his position would have quit – which constituted constructive discharge.

But other targets are less successful in constructive discharge claims that involve workplace bullying.

In *Aldridge v. Daikin America Inc.*, 2005 U.S. Dist. LEXIS 27389 (N.D. Ala. Oct. 6, 2005)), a federal judge ruled that a member of the Army National Guard who quit his job after a workplace altercation could not claim constructive discharge. The plaintiff demonstrated that he was the target of negative comments regarding his National Guard service, and that he was under a closer watch than were other employees. Yet, the Court found the plaintiff's "work conditions were not so intolerable that a reasonable person would have resigned... [Plaintiff] may have been under a closer watch than other...employees. He also may have been the target of negative comments... He was not, however, forced to resign from his job."

An employer generally may defend itself against a claim of constructive discharge by showing that it had installed a readily accessible and effective policy for reporting and resolving complaints of sexual harassment, and that the plaintiff unreasonably failed to avail him or herself of that employer-provided preventive or remedial apparatus.

No Magic Bullet

What the above cases show is that there is no magic bullet for targets of workplace bullying who are unfairly fired. That's why workplace anti-bully advocates are seeking new protections for good workers who are targeted by bullies. But pending further changes in the law, a claim of wrongful termination based upon a contract violation or a firing in violation of a public policy are one of many possible – though not ideal - avenues of redress.

16. BULLYING AND TORT LAW

"All cruelty springs from weakness." - Seneca, 4BC-AD65

A. Intentional Infliction of Emotional Distress

If there was a competition for the most outrageous instance of workplace bullying, this might be the winner:

Prosper, Inc., a Utah company that specializes in business coaching, was sued by an employee who was *literally* tortured during a motivational exercise.

In May 2007, Joshua Christopherson, a Prosper sales executive, led his team of salespeople to a nearby hilltop. He asked for a volunteer with "loyalty and determination" to participate in a "new motivational exercise." Chad Hudgens stepped up. Christopherson had Hudgens lie down, with his head pointed downhill. Christopherson then ordered other employees to hold down Hudgens arms and legs while Christopherson poured water from a gallon jug over Hudgens' mouth and nose. The process is known as waterboarding – a form of torture that simulates drowning and dates back to the Spanish Inquisition.

'Now guys," Christopherson told his sales crew, "you see how hard Chad was struggling for a breath of air, how hard he was trying to breathe? That's how hard I want you to go get back on the phones and make some sales. "

Christopherson used other unorthodox management techniques. According to court records, Christopherson would draw a mustache on an employee's face – using permanent marker –if the employee failed to meet performance goals. Christopherson patrolled the employees' work area with a wooden paddle, which he would use to strike desks and tabletops.

After the waterboarding incident, Hudgens said he suffered sleeplessness, anxiety, depression, and began to feel sick to his stomach at work. He sought psychological counseling and finally quit his job. Hudgens sued Prosper Inc. and Christopherson for common law assault and battery, intentional infliction of emotional distress, wrongful termination, and intentional interference with a contractual relationship.

But Utah Judge Gary Stott granted Prosper's motion to dismiss Hudgens's complaint on the grounds that it failed to state a valid claim. Judge Stott said Christopherson had used "poor judgment," but Stott reasoned that the purpose of Christopherson's exercise was not to injure Hudgens but to motivate his team members.

The Utah Supreme Court in 2010 reversed Judge Stott's ruling but on a technicality. The state's high court said that Judge

Stott abused his discretion by refusing to permit Hudgens to amend his complaint. (See *Hudgens v. Prosper Inc.,* No. 20090391 (Utah 11/23/10).

The Hudgens case demonstrates the limitations of tort law in workplace abuse cases. If a victim of torture can't successfully claim intentional infliction of emotional distress, who can?

Civil Wrong

A "tort" is basically a personal injury. It is defined as civil wrong – other than a breach of contract –that is recognized under the law as the grounds for a lawsuit. The commission of a tort results in a harm for which the injured party typically seeks monetary damages in civil court. Generally, damages for torts include:

- Compensatory damages or damages that pay, or compensate, an injured person for being harmed, including mental pain and anguish and any physical bodily harm attributable to the defendant's actions, reasonable and necessary medical expenses, economic losses, lost income or wages, diminution of earning capacity and even loss of consortium. Future damages can be awarded so long as there is a "reasonable probability" they will be sustained in the future.

- Nominal damages. If a plaintiff can't show financial loss, the jury can award nominal damages, which involve a small amount of money that the defendant must pay in order to show that the defendant was wrong.

– Punitive damages may be awarded to punish a defendant whose actions were malicious, willful, or outrageous.

In the absence of workplace anti-bully laws, targets of workplace bullying often look to the common law tort of Intentional Infliction of Emotional Distress (IIED). This is especially true for targets who lack protected status under state and federal discrimination laws.

Outrageous!

IIED is known as the "tort of outrage." But there is considerable debate about what constitutes outrage. This is particularly true when it comes to the workplace, where many judges believe that emotional distress is a normal part of the workplace environment. Courts traditionally have set incredibly high standards for what constitutes IIED.

One court found that to qualify as IIED, the conduct must be "so extreme in degree, as to go beyond all possible bounds of decency, and to be regarded as atrocious, and utterly intolerable in a civilized community... but does not extend to mere insults, indignities, threats, annoyances, petty oppressions, or other trivialities." (*Porter v. Bankers Life & Casualty Co.,* 2002 U.S. Dist. LEXIS 20627, at 5-6 (N.D. Ill. Oct. 25, 2002)).

A legal definition of the tort of IIED is:

"One who by extreme and outrageous conduct intentionally or recklessly causes severe emotional distress to another is subject to liability for such emotional distress, and if bodily harm to the other results from it, for such bodily harm."

This definition can be difficult to apply to a workplace bully. A bully typically intends to and does cause severe emotional distress, but does so through manipulation and deceit that erodes the target's reputation and self-esteem over time. There is often no "Ah ha!" moment rather there is a series of small blows that add up to a crippling wound. Consequently, courts often rule that the element of "extreme and outrageous" conduct is lacking in workplace bullying lawsuits.

But American society increasingly is becoming aware of the toll of workplace bullying on individuals, employers and society in general. And consequently, courts are becoming more receptive to IIED claims in relation to workplace bullying.

Bullying Could be IIED

An important legal development with respect to workplace bullying occurred in 2008 when the Indiana Supreme Court said that workplace bullying could be considered a form of IIED.

The Indiana Supreme Court, in *Raess v. Doescher*, 883 N.E.2d 790, 799 (Ind. 2008), ruled that the phrase "workplace bullying" is "like other general terms used to characterize a person's behavior, ... an entirely appropriate consideration in determining the issues before the jury ... workplace bullying could be considered a form of intentional infliction of emotional distress." The Court's comment came in an appeal challenging the introduction of trial testimony by an "expert" witness who called the defendant a workplace bully.

In *Raess*, Joseph E. Doescher, a medical technician at St. Francis Hospital in Beech Grove, IN, resigned as chief perfusionist to protest Dr. Daniel H. Raess' treatment of technical staff. Doescher, however, remained at the hospital as a staff perfusionist. A month later, Doescher assisted Dr. Raess, who was a cardiovascular surgeon, in surgery.

According to Doescher's lawsuit, the two men argued. Dr. Raess became irate and "aggressively and rapidly advanced on the plaintiff with clenched fists, piercing eyes, beet-red face, popping veins, and screaming and swearing at him." Fearing imminent physical harm, Doescher backed up against the wall and held up his hands to shield his face. Instead of striking Doescher, Dr. Raess turned and stormed out of the room. "You're finished," said Dr. Raess, "You're history."

Doescher left the hospital and never returned. He said he developed a panic disorder and depression, limiting his ability to perform under pressure in an operating room.

The jury dismissed Doescher's claim of IIED but ruled in his favor on a claim for assault. Doescher was awarded $325,000 in damages.

Dr. Raess appealed the verdict on the grounds that the trial court improperly admitted testimony by Gary Namie, the founder of the Workplace Bullying Institute, which characterized Dr. Raess as a workplace bully. Raess' attorney argued that Namie was not qualified to be an expert on workplace bullying because he is not a clinical psychologist and that Namie based his testimony on a telephone call with the plaintiff – without ever speaking to the defendant.

The Indiana Court of Appeals agreed that the trial court committed reversible error by admitting Namie's testimony and overturned the jury award.

In a 4-to-1 opinion, the Indiana Supreme Court reinstated the jury's award on a technicality, without really addressing whether Namie's testimony should have been allowed. One of the justices in the majority said that even if Namie's testimony was improper it was harmless error because the jury ultimately rejected the plaintiff's IIED claim.

In a scathing dissent, Justice Theodore R. Boehm, said Namie's testimony was highly prejudicial and not at all harmless. He said evidentiary rules permit expert opinion testimony as to scientific, technical, or other specialized knowledge to assist the trier of fact to understand the evidence or to determine a fact in issue. "Nowhere ... does Dr. Namie explain what a workplace bully is. Dr. Namie by his own testimony is not a clinical psychologist and is not qualified to testify as to how workplace bullying affected the plaintiff... Without any context, the 'workplace bullying' label is nothing more than highly prejudicial name-calling of no help to the jury."

As the *Raess* case demonstrates, the tort of IIED in the context of workplace bullying is a relatively new concept that will undoubtedly be the subject of future legal arguments. The case represents an important step forward, however, because it clearly acknowledges that workplace bullying can cause IIED.

A claim of IIED also was affirmed by the Texas Supreme Court in *GTE Southwest, Inc. v. Bruce*, 998 S.W.2d 605, 613-14 (Tex. 1999). In that case, a jury $275,000 to three workers whose supervisor repeatedly shouted profanities at them, physically charged them, pounded his fists and threatened them with termination during a two-year period.

Medications Denied

More recently, the Oklahoma Supreme Court upheld a claim of IIED in a case involving a fast-food worker who was bullied when his supervisor repeatedly denied him permission to take anti-seizure medication. (See *Durham v. McDonald's Restaurants of Oklahoma, Inc.*, No. 108193 (Okla. May 24, 2011)).

Camran Durham, 16, said that his supervising manager denied three requests to take prescription anti-seizure medication. This made Durham fearful that he would suffer a seizure. After the manager called him a "f...ing retard," Durham ran out the door crying. Durham said fellow students at his high school began repeating the manager's comment and he became "withdrawn" and "a recluse." Durham's mother said he eventually refused to leave the house and had to be home-schooled.

Lower courts agreed with McDonald's Restaurant that the manager's conduct did not rise to the level of "extreme and outrageous." But the Oklahoma Supreme Court, in its 6-3 ruling, disagreed and remanded the case for further proceedings.

Oklahoma's high court said Durham was a victim of IIED: "The test is whether the conduct is so extreme in degree as to go beyond all possible bounds of decency, and is atrocious and utterly intolerable in a civilized community .... [W]e find that the manager's use of "f...ing retard" in addressing a minor employee who is filled with apprehension after being denied permission to take anti-seizure medication may reasonably be regarded as meeting this test."

IIED and Workers' Compensation

Exclusivity provisions of state workers' compensation laws generally bar lawsuits involving work-related injuries, including psychological injuries. Therefore, targets of IIED may be unable to file an IIED lawsuit. But some courts have ruled that a plaintiff can file an IIED lawsuit if the employer *intentionally* caused the injury.

In a 2-1 decision, an appellate court ruled in *Subbe-Hirt v. Baccigalupi,* 94 F.3d 111 (1996), that a plaintiff could get around the exclusivity provision of the New Jersey Workers' Compensation Act by showing the employer's deliberate intention to inflict emotional distress. The plaintiff, Elaine J. Subbe-Hirt, a salesperson, presented evidence to show that her boss, Robert Baccigalupi, intended to cause her harm. The court's ruling meant that Subbe-Hirt was not limited merely to compensatory damages under the state's workers' compensation law -- she could sue for much more lucrative punitive damages.

Subbe-Hirt alleged that:

– Baccigalupi replaced females' given names with the term "cunt" to depersonalize and deride the women in the office;

– He asked Subbe-Hirt for her resignation almost every time she was in his office and even kept an unsigned resignation on his desk;

– He would "grill" her about her work and then call her clients and say – in front of her – "Elaine says this; what do you say?"

– After one meeting with Baccigalupi, Subbe-Hirt said she "literally blacked out behind the wheel and hit a tractor trailer just from stress and emotion ..." She suffered severe injuries that required eight days of hospitalization.

– Subbe-Hirt's psychiatrist said Baccigalupi's badgering and intimidation caused Subbe-Hurt to be totally disabled with post-traumatic stress disorder.

Key evidence in the case was a note that Subbe-Hirt presented to Baccigalupi from her psychiatrist stating she should not be placed under undue stress. Baccigalupi allegedly refused to place the note in her personnel file, and continued his abusive behavior.

The judicial majority said Baccigalupi's conduct was sufficiently outrageous to support her claim of IIED.

Another issue that frequently arises with respect to IIED claims is whether the claim is sufficiently distinct to stand on its own. In Title VII discrimination cases, for example, an employer may argue that an IIED claim is usurped by the discrimination claim. In other words, the discrimination caused the emotional distress and, therefore, the plaintiff should not be allowed to assert a separate claim for IIED and collect additional damages. The U.S. District Court of Appeals for the Seventh Circuit rejected that theory in an Illinois case, *Naeem v. McKesson Drug Company*, 444 F.3d 593 (7th Cir. 2006).

This is Extreme!

Sally Naeem began her career at McKeeson, a wholesale distributor of pharmaceuticals, as a keypunch operator in 1978. By 1992, she had worked her way up to computer room supervisor at the company's Romeoville, Illinois distribution center. She agreed in 1993 to assume the role of transportation coordinator, a full-time job, while continuing to serve as computer- room supervisor. In March 1994, Naeem complained to HR that her manager had sexually propositioned her. Naeem's promising career began a steep decline; she was passed over for a promotion four months later in favor of a male employee.

Naeem became pregnant with her fourth child in 1995. It was a difficult pregnancy and she suffered from gestational diabetes, hypertension and other complications. Despite this, she said her workload greatly increased. Among other things, she said she was required to climb up a metal stairway onto a raised mezzanine level and to crawl under furniture to set up computers.

Naeem was fired for alleged performance issues in 1996. She subsequently filed a federal lawsuit alleging sexual discrimination under Title VII and IIED.

At the trial, Naeem's husband said Naeem was unable to eat, experienced crying spells and could not breast feed her newborn. After being fired, he said that Naeem began to consider suicide. Her family encouraged her to see a psychiatrist. Naeem was diagnosed with Post Traumatic Stress Disorder and major depressive disorder. She was never able to find an equivalent job and eventually took work as an entry level computer operator.

The jury ruled against Naeem on the Title VII claim, but found in her favor on the IIED claim. She was awarded $495,000 in damages, including $250,000 for pain and suffering. On appeal, however, the defendant argued that the IIED claim could not stand in the face of the dismissal of the Title VII claim.

The federal appellate court said Naeem's claim of IIED was an independent tort that was distinct from her charge of discrimination. The Court agreed that the defendant's behavior was sufficiently extreme to merit the jury's finding of IIED. "[I]t is clear that her claim rests not just on behavior that is sexually harassing, but rather behavior that would be a tort no matter what the motives of the defendant," the Court concluded.

B. Negligent Infliction of Emotional Distress

Some states also recognize the tort of Negligent Infliction of Emotional Distress (NIED), which covers situations in which the employer's conduct created an unreasonable risk of emotional distress. The distress must be foreseeable and severe enough to cause illness or bodily harm. The plaintiff also must show that the defendant's conduct caused the stress.

The Court of Appeals of Washington held that Gina Strong could sue a school district for NIED in *Strong v. Terrell*, 147 Wn. App. 376 (2008). A member of the Public School Employees of Washington union, Strong worked as a printing press operator in a print shop supervised by James Terrell. Strong claimed Terrell verbally abused her daily, told "blonde jokes" and ridiculed her personal life. He allegedly spit in her face and, after assigning her to a night shift as punishment, routed the telephone to an automatic answering machine. Strong said Terrell's behavior caused her to vomit and experience anxiety attacks, depression, and heart palpitations. The appeals court found that Strong's claim did not stem from a disciplinary action or a personality dispute, and that her allegedly abusive treatment led to a medical diagnosis. The Court concluded that a jury could find that Terrell's actions constituted NIED.

The primary aim of tort law is to provide relief for the damages suffered by the plaintiff and to deter others from committing the same type of harms. The injured person may sue for an injunction to halt the tortuous conduct or for monetary damages.

C. Assault

As demonstrated by the *Raess* case cited earlier in this chapter (*See* IIED), a target of workplace bullying may prevail on a claim of assault. An assault is a tort that occurs when the perpetrator intentionally puts another person in reasonable apprehension of imminent harmful or offensive contact – The plaintiff is not required to show the perpetrator intended to cause physical injury, and no physical injury need occur. The plaintiff must show that defendant desired or was substantially certain that his or her action would cause the apprehension of immediate harmful or offensive contact.

Even though the cardiovascular surgeon in the *Raess* case never actually struck the medical technician, the surgeon's actions placed the medical technician in fear of imminent bodily injury, which the jury found sufficient to constitute the tort of assault and to support an award of $325,000.

The state can criminally prosecute intentional torts, such as assault, battery and false imprisonment.

D. Invasion of Privacy

Supreme Court Justice Louis Brandeis once remarked that the right to privacy is "the right to be let alone ... the right most valued by civilized men." (*Olmstead v. United States*, 277 U.S. 438 (1928)).

Some courts recognize that employees have a limited right to privacy in the workplace and that if an employee is fired on the basis of information obtained through an invasion of privacy, the employee's discharge is wrongful.

The Restatement (Second) of Torts recognizes four common law torts for invasion of privacy:

- Intrusion upon one's seclusion or private concerns, physical or otherwise;
- Public disclosure of private facts causing injury to one's reputation;
- Publicly placing an individual in a false light, and;
- Appropriation of another's name or likeness for one's own use or benefit.

A privacy tort that is commonly invoked in employment cases is intrusion upon seclusion.

In *Johnson v. K Mart Corporation*, 723 N.E.2d 1192 (2000), an Illinois appellate court reversed a lower court's dismissal of a case that involved spying on employees. Fifty-five Kmart workers alleged their privacy rights were violated when K. Mart hired private investigators to work undercover as employees to investigate theft, vandalism and drug use by regular employees. The investigators filed their reports with information about employee family matters, such as domestic violence and impending divorces. The detectives reported the sexual conduct of employees, including the number and gender of sexual partners and health-related issues, including one employee's prostate problems. They characterized certain employees as alcoholics because they drank "frequently."

In its ruling, the appeals Court recognized the tort of invasion of privacy by intrusion upon exclusion. The Court said the tort contains four elements:

- An unauthorized intrusion or prying into the plaintiff's seclusion;
- An intrusion that is offensive or objectionable to a reasonable person;
- The matter upon which the intrusion occurs is private; and
- The intrusion causes anguish and suffering.

The Court recognized that the plaintiffs had voluntarily disclosed private information to the investigators but said that: "A disclosure obtained through deception cannot be said to be a truly voluntary disclosure. Plaintiffs had a reasonable expectation that their conversations with 'coworkers' would remain private, at least to the extent that intimate life details would not be published to their employer." Furthermore, the Court said Kmart admitted it had "no business purpose" for collecting such private information about their employees but never told the investigators to stop collecting the information.

E. Public Disclosure of Private Facts

The Court also recognized a second tort involving invasion of privacy- the public disclosure of private facts. The Court said this tort requires the plaintiff to prove that:

– Publicity was given to the disclosure of private facts;

– The facts were private and not public facts; and

– The matter made public would be highly offensive to a reasonable person.

"The evidence shows that personal details about plaintiffs' private lives were disclosed to their employer by the investigators. We find that these facts raise a genuine issue as to whether publicity was given to private facts," said the Court.

F. Defamation

In the employment context, defamation is any false statement about an employee communicated by an employer to a third party that harms that employee's reputation or deters others from dealing with the employee in a business setting. Defamation arises when an employer intentionally defames an employee by accusing him or her of a crime (i.e. stealing) to justify firing him or her. It also occurs when a former employer makes untrue statements about a former employee to another employee or the public. Defamation is frequently asserted when a former employer gives false information to a prospective employer.

Truth, of course, is a defense against defamation.

The tort of defamation includes both libel and slander. Libel was traditionally considered defamation by written or printed words. Slander consists of the communication of a defamatory statement by spoken words or by transitory gestures.

Four elements are generally required to show defamation:

1. A false statement purporting to be fact concerning another person or entity;

2. Publication or communication of that statement to a third person;

3. Intent or at least negligence on the part of the person making the statement;

4. Some harm caused to the person or entity who is the subject of the statement.

If the defamation occurs in the midst of a labor dispute, the Plaintiff also may be required to prove the Defendant acted with "actual malice." – or with knowledge that the communication was false or with reckless disregard for whether the communication was true or false. These types of cases often involve materials and letters dispatched during union organizing campaigns containing charges and counter-charges.

Post Termination Comments

Defamation often emerges as an issue in the context of employee termination.

In *Corey v. Pierce County*, 154 Wn. App. 752 (2010), the Court of Appeals of Washington affirmed a $3 million award for defamation and Intentional Infliction of Emotional Distress (IIED) in connection with termination proceedings involving a 30-year deputy prosecutor.

The deputy prosecutor encountered difficulties when she attempted to transfer a subordinate from the department's sexual assault unit to another unit. The Plaintiff's boss, the Pierce County Prosecuting Attorney, became concerned about the deputy prosecutor's ability to communicate and eventually took steps to fire her. She resigned.

After she left, the county discovered money in her desk that had been raised for a colleague whose child was ill. The local newspaper published an article quoting her boss as stating that he had lost confidence in her. Furthermore, he said that she was subject to a "criminal investigation" regarding the money in her desk. The Plaintiff said the article caused her to become severely depressed, suicidal, and that she could not find another legal position. She sued for defamation and IIED.

The Washington appeals court said her supervisor's statements to the press established sufficient evidence for defamation and false light claims because he knew that an internal investigation had not revealed any improper conduct. The Court said the defendant essentially accused the plaintiff of criminal behavior and that such accusation created a viable claim for IIED.

Indirectly Identified Workers

Similarly, in *Ball v. Taylor*, 416 F. 3d 915 (2005), a federal appeals court in Iowa refused to dismiss a defamation lawsuit brought by 58 employees of Titan Tire Corp. Maurice Taylor, Jr., a principal in Titan, held a press conference in which he accused the employees of filing fraudulent disability claims for hearing loss. He said Titan planned to file a racketeering lawsuit against the employees and the United Steelworkers of America. The Court rejected the company's defense that it could not be held liable because it accused the employees as a group. "Although Taylor did not state the employees' names individually, he ... stated he was suing them because they had committed fraud, then handed his audience copies of the complaint, which identified the individual employees by name in the caption and contained their names, addresses, and positions in an appendix," said the Court.

Occasionally, a defamation lawsuit is filed by a current employee against a supervisor – this can be a risky proposition.

Lawrence J. Connell, a tenured associate professor at Widener Law School in Delaware, sued his boss, Dean Linda L. Ammons, and two students for defamation in 2011. Connell alleged that Ammons, during administrative proceedings, made false statements that characterized Connell as racist and sexist.

Two students initially complained to Ammons about Connell's depiction of Ammons in a teaching hypothetical. Connell portrayed himself as a perpetrator who tried to shoot the dean in a dispute about a parking space. Connell, who had taught at the law school for 26 years, said Ammons exploited the incident in an attempt to fire him because of his conservative political beliefs.

After learning of Connell's teaching hypothetical, Ammons asked that Connell be suspended for a year, banned from the campus and ordered to undergo a psychiatric evaluation. The parties settled the lawsuit in 2012. According to a statement by Connell's attorney: "[A]ll claims amongst all parties have been resolved amicably and *Professor Connell's employment with the University and Law School has been concluded*." (Emphasis added.)

Damages for defamation may include general injury to reputation, mental suffering, alienation of associates, specific items of pecuniary loss, or whatever form of harm would be recognized by state tort law. A defendant can be held liable for damages "per se" – which means that damages are presumed – if the defendant falsely accuses someone a criminal offense, a loathsome disease, serious sexual misconduct or misconduct that is incompatible with his business, trade or office.

G. False Imprisonment

The classic case of false imprisonment in the employment context occurs when an employer's "loss prevention experts" call an employee who is suspected of theft into a back room and then interrogates the employee about stolen merchandise.

265

False imprisonment is an intentional tort in which the perpetrator restrains another person without having the legal right to do so. This can mean physical restraint – such as tying a person to a chair – but physical force is not required. Threats of immediate physical force are sufficient to be acts of restraint. Accidental confinement is not considered false imprisonment.

According to the Restatement (Second) of Torts, a defendant is subject to liability for false imprisonment if:

- He or she intends to confine the other or a third person within boundaries fixed by the actor, and;
- The act directly or indirectly results in such a confinement of the other, and;
- The other is conscious of the confinement or is harmed by it.

An area of confinement is considered "bounded" – or closed off to escape – if freedom of movement is limited in all directions or the other person does not know that there is a means of escape. False imprisonment is not the same as preventing another from going in a particular direction in which s/he has a right or privilege to go. In that case, the area is not considered closed off to escape.

The tort of false imprisonment requires the perpetrator to intentionally confine the other person even if s/he does not intend to harm the other person.

Prank Goes Awry

In *Fuerschbach v. Southwest Airlines Co.*, 439 F. 3d 1197 (10th Cir. 2006), a supposedly good-natured prank went awry. Southwest Airlines, which calls itself a "fun loving, spirited company" had a tradition in which pranks were played on new employees who have completed their probationary period. Marcie Fuerschbach worked as a customer service representative serving travelers at Southwest's main ticket counter in Albuquerque.

Fuerschbach was approached by two armed Albuquerque police officers and told that she was under arrest for an outstanding warrant. They demanded that she take off her badges and handed them to her supervisor, who was standing nearby. The officers placed Fuerschbach's hands behind her back and handcuffed her. One of the officers said to Fuerschbach, who was crying, "We don't want to embarrass you anymore so we'll take you to the elevator so we don't have to walk in front of all those people." Fifteen feet from the elevator, someone jumped out and yelled, "Congratulations for being off probation!"

Fuerschbach was not amused. She began seeing a psychiatrist, who diagnosed her with post-traumatic stress. Fuerschbach filed a lawsuit against the airlines, her supervisors, the city of Albuquerque and the police officers, alleging, among other things, false imprisonment. The city and the police officers asked to be dropped from the lawsuit on the grounds of qualified immunity. The Court denied their request, finding the officers lacked probable cause to restrain Fuerschbach in handcuffs and to direct her movements. The Court said it was not relevant that the tort was characterized as a prank or "even a good faith but incorrect belief that the tort victim will enjoy the joke."

Another type of false imprisonment was alleged in a case involving a cash register clerk at a Costco warehouse in San Marcos, California. Mary Pytelewski, a 10-year Costco employee, filed a class action lawsuit against the store in 2009. She said Costco locked in employees against their will at closing time for 15 minutes or more while managers removed jewelry from cases and checked cash registers. She alleged false imprisonment and a denial of wages. According to news reports, Pytelewski was "rebuffed and ridiculed at every turn" when she complained about the practice. She was then was given a negative evaluation and a supervisor was assigned to her cash register at closing time to watch her. The lawsuit, which seeks $50 million in damages, was expected to go to trial in 2012.

H. Negligent Hiring

The tort of Negligent Hiring is often invoked when an employer hires a violent felon or sex offender and puts the individual in a position where he or she can cause harm to others. An employer can be held liable if the employer knows or should have known, at the time of hiring, about an applicant's particular unfitness for a job, which created an unreasonable risk of harm to the others. An employer has a duty to maintain a safe environment by taking steps to protect those whom the employer might reasonably anticipate would be injured by the employee. The doctrine is derived from the common law fellow-servant rule, which imposed a duty on employers to select employees who would not endanger fellow employees by their presence on the job. The basic elements of a cause of action for Negligent Hiring are:

- The employee must have a legal duty to use due care;

- There must be a breach of that duty;

- The breach must be reasonably foreseeable and the proximate cause of the plaintiff's injury

Courts determine the existence and scope of the employer's duty by balancing the nature of the job and the foreseeability of harm. For example, in *Gaines v. Monsanto Co.*, 655 SW.2d 568, 570 (Mo. App. 1983), the Court held that knowingly hiring a convicted rapist to work in the mail room, where he would circulate among female employees, could subject the company to liability for negligent hiring, because the ex-felon later murdered a female co-worker in her apartment.

Conversely, in *Worstell Parking Inc. v. Aisada*, 442 S.E.2d 469 (Ga. App. 1994), the Court said an employer who hired a parking lot attendant who had a conviction for a drug-related offense was not responsible when the attendant later assaulted a customer because the attendant's drug conviction did not indicate a propensity for violence.

A related theory −Negligent Supervision/Retention− holds that the employer can be liable if it knew or should have known of an employee's unfitness, which endangered others, but retained the employee anyway and failed to take corrective action through coaching, reassignment or termination.

In *Daka, Inc. v. McCrae*, 839 A.2d 682 (D.C. 2003), Tyrone McCrae, a male banquet chef complained that he was sexually harassed by a male supervisor, the catering director, after refusing the supervisor's dinner invitation. McCrae was subsequently demoted and fired. McCrae sued for negligent supervision and retaliation. The trial court found the evidence was overwhelming that Daka flagrantly ignored McCrae's pleas for help and that the wrongdoing inflicted upon McCrae was severe and was exacerbated by the defendant's failure to conduct even a rudimentary investigation into the allegations of harassment. The jury awarded McCrae $187,500 in compensatory damages and $4.8 million in punitive damages. The Court of Appeals for the District of Columbia upheld the jury's verdict but vacated the punitive damage award as excessive. The appeal court instructed the trial court to reduce punitive damages in a manner consistent with case law.

I. Negligent Retention

In *Yunker v. Honeywell, Inc.*, 496 NW 2d 419 (1993), a Minnesota appeals court made a distinction between negligent hiring and negligent retention. This case involved the murder of an employee by a co-worker after he had already murdered another co-worker at the same company a few years earlier.

Honeywell Corporation employed Randy Landin for about two years in the 1970s until he was sent to prison for strangling and murdering a co-worker. Landin was released from prison in 1984 and Honeywell rehired him to work as a janitor. Kathleen Nessler was assigned to work on Landin's maintenance crew. When Nessler rebuffed Landin's sexual advances, he began to harass her. She sought help from a supervisor and requested a transfer. On July 1, 1988, Nessler found a death threat scratched on her locker door. Landin did not go to work after July 1, 1998 and resigned from Honeywell on July 11, 1988. A week later, Nessler was found lying dead on her driveway. Landin was convicted of killing Nessler with a close-range shotgun blast.

The Court rejected a claim of Negligent Hiring brought by Nessler's estate but said Honeywell could be held liable for the tort of Negligent Retention.

The first part of the Court's reasoning was that employers would not hire any ex-felon if courts ruled that all ex-felons are inherently dangerous, and that all harmful acts by ex-felons are automatically foreseeable to employers. In this case, the Court said, Landin was hired as a maintenance worker whose job did not involve exposure to the general public and only limited contact with co-workers. "Nessler was not a reasonably foreseeable victim at the time Landin was hired," the Court concluded.

But the Court said Honeywell could be held liable for Negligent Retention of Landin because there was evidence that he had demonstrated a propensity of abuse toward co-workers. Landin reportedly had sexually harassed female employees and had challenged a co-worker to a fight. The Court said Honeywell failed its duty of care to Nessler because it was foreseeable that retaining Landin, after he demonstrated a propensity for abuse, could put Nessler in harm's way. "This foreseeability gives rise to a duty of care to Nessler that is not outweighed by policy considerations of employment opportunity (for ex-felons)," wrote the Court.

J. Tortuous Interference/ Contract

Generally, tort liability may be imposed on a person who intentionally and improperly interferes with the performance of a contract between another and a third person. Arguably, a bullying supervisor acts outside the scope of his or her employment to interfere with the target's employment relationship with the employer.

The tort of intentional interference with a business relationship dates back to an 1853 English case, *Lymley v. Gye*, in which a singer, Johanna Wagner, was hired by Benjamin Lumley to sing exclusively at Her Majesty's Theatre for three months. Frederick Gye, who ran the competing Covent Garden Theatre, induced Wagner to break her contract with by promising to pay her more. An injunction was issued to prevent her singing at Covent Garden but Gye persuaded her to disregard it. Lumley successfully sued Gye for the income he had lost. The Court found that Gye had wrongfully and maliciously enticing Wagner to break her contract with Lumley.

To recover under a theory of tortuous interference with a business relationship, a plaintiff generally must establish that the defendant acted improperly, with malice and intent to injure and induced a third party or parties not to enter into or continue a business relationship with the plaintiff. These cases often turn upon the intent of the defendant.

In *Tenge v. Phillips Modern Ag Co.,* 446 F.3d 903 (8th Cir. Iowa 2006),a federal judge affirmed the dismissal of a case filed by Madelynn Tenge, an employee-at-will for a company run by a husband and wife. Tenge was fired because the wife suspected her of having an affair with the husband. The Court said an at-will employee may maintain a tortuous interference claim if the plaintiff presents "substantial evidence that the defendant's predominate or sole motive of the interference was to damage the plaintiff." The Court acknowledged that the wife had retaliated against Tenge but said "Tenge's own testimony undermines the proposition that Lori's 'predominate or sole motive' in terminating Tenge's employment was to damage Tenge, rather than to preserve her marriage."

One Arrow in the Quiver

Tort law clearly is not the complete answer to workplace bullying. With respect to IIED, bullying rarely meets the daunting level of outrage required by courts. Defamation and false imprisonment are useful but only if the facts of the case fit the specific elements of the torts. Negligent Hiring and Negligent Retention are most successful when targets can show they suffered a physical rather than an emotional injury from a co-worker.

Like the other causes of action listed in this book, torts are arrows in a quiver that can be used by targets of bullying. Not every arrow will hit its mark but some might. And, in the absence of a specific workplace anti-bully law, what other choices do targets of bullying have?

CONCLUSION

What does it really mean to *survive* bullies, queen bees and psychopaths in the workplace? The preceding pages are devoted to laws and legal strategies but survival does not depend upon a court victory.

There is no federal or state law at present that directly addresses workplace bullying and few targets have the emotional or financial wherewithal to wage a lengthy and uncertain court battle. Federal courts tend to be hostile to employment lawsuits brought by workers; these types of cases are more likely than other cases to be dismissed on pre- or post- trial motions by a judge before they ever reach a jury. Given the obstacles, winning a court case involving workplace bullying can seem more like serendipity than a triumph of justice. Conversely, losing such a case may reflect more upon societal ignorance of the problem of workplace bullying than the merits of the case.

The meaning of survival in the context of workplace bullying is far simpler than a favorable jury verdict. Targets win when they survive with their sense of psychological and mental well-being reasonably intact.

A bully is like a bored child pressing a fat thumb down on an ant crossing the pavement on a hot summer afternoon. The bully's goal is to extinguish the target's sense of self respect and dignity. No amount of subservience is enough – only absolute and unquestioning subservience. Bullies do not stop until the target waves the white flag of surrender or is ousted from the workplace.

Workplace bullying is a recognized form of workplace violence and it does tremendous violence to a target's spirit. It is described by some targets as a form of terrorism. Bullying shares the same roots as intimate partner abuse, child abuse and elder abuse. One party is attempting to gain improper power and coercive control over the other, using common tactics of fear, blaming, manipulation, lies, humiliation, etc. A target who is severely bullied suffers potentially severe physical and psychological injuries.

Because the United States has been so slow to recognize workplace bullying as a problem, many targets do not understand what is happening to them. When they finally do realize they are being bullied, it can be a tremendous source of relief. Often they can see the universal signs and patterns of bullying. They can see that it is a problem that afflicts one in every three or four workers. They are not alone, and they are not at fault.

Being bullied is like being lost in a nightmarish circus funhouse. For weeks, months or years, targets experience work as if they are stumbling through dark hallways with tilted floors, a confusing maze of mirrors, blasts of blinding lights, and rooms with odd angles. A target's sense of reality may become more distorted with each episode of abuse. Some targets are so beaten down that they come to believe the bully and blame themselves.

When targets do understand the dynamics of workplace bullying, their uncertainty, confusion and fear begin to disappear like a fog in the afternoon sun. Instead of reeling from one crisis to another, they can step back and analyze the situation and respond in an effective manner. They can make a choice to refuse to allow the bully to inflict any more damage to their sense of self and well-being. They can reclaim their power, which was stolen by the bully and, in the process, deprive the bully of his or her victory.

Given the current state of the law, it may not be realistic for targets to pin their hopes on holding on to the same job with the same company. Targets must survey their options and pick the course of action that makes the most sense for them. If complaining to the employer fails to remedy the problem, some targets may be better off looking for a new job or accepting their losses and walking away. That's a choice; not a defeat. But some workers do not have the option of quitting or finding a new employer. They may hold a unique job, face the prospect of age discrimination or they may be part of a two wage-earning family with strong ties to a community. For them, it may make more sense to seek a transfer within the company to a position outside the bully's control or to consult with an employment lawyer about exploring legal options.

To put the problem in perspective, workplace bullying is recognized in many industrialized countries as a type of violence that is equivalent to physical violence. In Europe, for example, countries do not tolerate the kind of destructive workplace abuse that the legislatures and courts in the United States appear to consider to be a mundane and a routine part of working life. Workers in Europe have a basic right to dignity that extends to their workplace; employers have a responsibility to prevent and eliminate workplace bullying. And many industrialized countries interpret workplace health and safety laws to require employers to provide a workplace free from psychological violence and bullying.

Not so in America. At present, the United States leaves its workers at the mercy of bullies, queen bees and psychopaths.

Despite a decade of grassroots efforts, there is no state law at present that specifically addresses workplace bullying. A state may eventually adopt such a law. It's possible that other states will follow suit. But it will most likely take decades for a significant number of states to adopt workplace anti-bully laws and some states never will. Also, the proposed Healthy Workplace Bill does nothing to address the problem of strategic harassment by employers to achieve an organizational goal (i.e., dismissing a good employee who may file a worker's compensation claim to avoid paying benefits).

With all due respect to Suffolk Law School Professor David C. Yamada, author of the proposed Healthy Workplace Bill, and the Workplace Bullying Institute, I submit that the problem of workplace bullying will not be solved in any meaningful way without a national, uniform law and/or regulations. That is why I co-launched a petition drive in 2012 asking the U.S. President and

U.S. Secretary of Labor to formulate proposed national workplace anti-bully legislation. (See, http://www.thepetitionsite.com/1/protect-us-workers /)

The petition generated thousands of signatures in a few short months, as well as many wrenching stories of targets who suffered severe trauma as a result of bullying on the job. Here are some of the comments:

- "I once worked in an abusive workplace. My co-worker killed himself. I think fairly often about whether I could have stopped it."

- "Workplace bullying is a living death for the victims. PTSD, depression, anxiety, suicide and physical health issues result when perpetual bullying is given free reign. Workplaces are not meant to be a haven for bullies ..."

- "I have been a victim of workplace bullying by a supervisor!! My only choice after talking to the HR department of this large corporation over and over again all in a 4-year period was to quit! There needs to be protection in the workplace against this kind of behavior!"

America has always been a beacon of freedom and hope to the oppressed around the world. How sad it is that the United States today lags behind other industrialized countries that require employers to maintain a workplace free from physical and psychological hazards. How ironic that workers in Europe have a legal right to be treated with respect and dignity in the workplace but not workers in America.

The United States' troubled economy means that millions of workers have little choice but to endure the day-to-day health-endangering battering of bullies, queen bees and psychopaths. To paraphrase Thomas Paine: "These are the times that try our souls." Many workers have drastically fewer employment opportunities and society's social safety net is becoming increasingly frayed. So targets are left to suffer well-documented short-term and long-term physical and psychological injuries caused by workplace bullying. Meanwhile, society spends billions each year to subsidize bullying employers. Taxpayers ultimately foot the bill for higher health care costs and social benefits (unemployment insurance, welfare, etc.

We need a revolution, not unlike the revolution of 1770s that freed Americans from the tyranny of English monarchs.

We need a new paradigm. Employment is a contract between the worker and the employer. Courts must not allow the employer to break the contract by preventing the employee from performing. In other words, employers must be held to a duty to prevent and stop bullying. A bullying supervisor sabotages a target and builds impediments to a target's success. Bullies prevent targets from successfully performing their jobs. Bullies drive targets out of the workplace.

Perhaps the most discouraging aspect of all of this is that bad employers are allowed to use strategic harassment to destroy a worker's financial security and health for pragmatic reasons.

Employers who "get rid of" good workers to avoid a legal duty –
like paying overtime or workers compensation –should face severe
consequences under the law.

The time is long, long overdue for the U.S. government to
act to protect the workers who built this country from the carnage
of unjust and needless workplace bullying.

Cases & Authorities

Cases

Aldridge v. Daikin America Inc., 2005 U.S. Dist. LEXIS 27389 (N.D. Ala. Oct. 6, 2005)

Alfano v. Costello, 294 F.3d 365, 373 (2d Cir. 2002)

Allen v. City of Chicago, 2011 WL 941383 (N.D. Ill. 2011)

Ampersand Publishing, LLC d/b/a Santa Barbara News-Press and Graphics Communications Conference International Brotherhood of Teamsters and Robert Guiliano, 31-CA-027950 (NLRB, August 11, 2011)

Ball v. Taylor, 416 F. 3d 915 (2005)

Bammert v. Don's SuperValu, Inc., 646 NW 2d 365 (2002)

Barrett v. Omaha National Bank, 726 F.2d 424 (1984)

Bracke v. County of L.A., 60 Fed. Appx. 120, 2003 U.S. App. LEXIS 4204 (9th Cir. 2003)

Brooks v. Hilton Casinos Inc., 959 F.2d 757, 7 (1992)

Clark v. O'Reilly Auto. Inc., No. 09-00851 (E.D. Ark, 5/23/11)

Corey v. Pierce County, 154 Wn. App. 752 (2010)

Crystal Princeton Refining Co., 222 N. L. R. B. 1068, 1069 (1976)

Daka, Inc. v. McCrae, 839 A.2d 682 (D.C. 2003)

Davis v. Monroe County Board of Education, 526 U.S. 629 (1999)

Dediol v. Best Chevrolet Inc., No. 10-30-767 (5th Cir. 9/12/2011)

Derr v. Gulf Oil Corp., 796 F.2d 340, 343-44 (10th Cir. 1986)

Durham v. McDonald's Restaurants of Oklahoma, Inc., No. 108193 (Okla. May 24, 2011)

EEOC v. Nat'l Educ. Ass'n, 422 F.3d 840 (2005) *Everson v. Michigan Dept. of Corrections*, 391 F.3d 737 (6th Cir. 2004)

Fu v. Owens, No. 09-2489, (8th Cir. 10/6/10)

Fuerschbach v. Southwest Airlines Co., 439 F. 3d 1197 (10th Cir. 2006)

Gaines v. Monsanto Co., 655 SW.2d 568, 570 (Mo. App. 1983)

Goss v. Exxon Office Systems Co., 747 F.2d 885, 888 (3d Cir. 1984)

GTE Southwest, Inc. v. Bruce, 998 S.W.2d 605, 613-14 (Tex. 1999)

Harris v. Forklift Sys. Inc., 510 U.S. 17 (1993) *Hayduk v. Johnstown*, 2010 WL 2650248 (3d Cir. July 2, 2010)

Honaker v. Smith, 256 F.3d 477 (7th Cir. 2001)

Johnson v. K Mart Corporation, 723 N.E.2d 1192 (2000)

Kasten v. Saint-Gobain Performance Plastic, 131 S.Ct. 1325 (2011)

Lin v. Great Rose Fashion, Inc., No. 09–834 (E.D.N.Y. June 3, 2009)

Love v. Motiva Enters. LLC, No. 08-30996, unpublished opinion (5th Cir. 10/16/09)

Margiotta v. Christian Hospital Northeast Northwest d/b/a Christian Hospital and BJC Health System, No. SC90249 (Mo. 2/9/2010) *Martin v. New York Life Insurance Co.*, 42 N.E. 416, 417 (N.Y. 1895)

McKelvey v. Secretary of United States Army, No. 10-1172 (6th Cir. Dec. 14, 2011)

Mendez v. Starwood Hotels & Resorts Worldwide, Inc., 2010 U.S. Dist. LEXIS 107709 (S.D.N.Y. Sept. 30, 2010)

Meritor Sav. Bank v. Vinson, 106 S. Ct. 2399 (1986)

Naeem v. McKesson Drug Company, 444 F.3d 593 (7th Cir. 2006)

NLRB v. Washington Aluminum Co., 370 U.S. 9, 14, 82 S.Ct. 1099, 8 L.Ed.2d 298 (1962)

Olmstead v. United States, 277 U.S. 438 (1928)

Oncale v. Sundowner Offshore Servs., Inc., 523 U.S. 75 (1998)

Pa. State Police v. Suders, 542 U.S. 129, 147 (2004)

Pappas v. J.S.B. Holdings Inc., 392 F. Supp. 2d 1095 (D. Ariz. 2005)

Patterson v. Hudson Area Schools, 724 F.Supp.2d 682 (2010)

Porter v. Bankers Life & Casualty Co., 2002 U.S. Dist LEXIS 20627, at 5-6 (N.D. Ill. Oct. 25, 2002)

Raess v. Doescher, 883 N.E.2d 790 (2008)

Schultz v. Advocate Health & Hospitals Corp., No. 01 C 0702 (N.D. Ill. 2002)

Scott v. Phoenix Schools, Inc., 75 Cal.App.4th 702 (2009)

Skaggs v. Kroger Co., No. 2:10-0768 (S.D.W. Va. 4/21/11)

Street et al v. U.S. Corrugated Inc., No. 1:08-cv-00153, (W.D.Ky. 2011)

Subbe-Hirt v. Baccigalupi, 94 F.3d 111 (1996)

Sutton v. Tomco Machining, Inc., 129 Ohio St.3d 153 (2011)

Tenge v. Phillips Modern Ag Co., 446 F.3d 903 (8th Cir. Iowa 2006)

Thompson v. North A. Stainless, LP, 130 S.Ct. 3542 (2011)

Tinker v. Des Moines Independent School District, 393 U.S. 503 (1969)

Toussaint v. Blue Cross and Blue Shield of Michigan, 292 N.W.2d 880 (Mich. 1980)

Worstell Parking Inc. v. Aisada, 442 S.E.2d 469 (Ga. App. 1994)

Yunker v. Honeywell, Inc., 496 NW 2d 419 (1993)

Authorities

A. Georgakopoulos et al, *Workplace Bullying: A Complex Problem in Contemporary Organizations,* 2 International Journal of Business and Social Science 3 (Special Issue – January 2011).

Adam D. Galinsky, et al., *Power and Perspectives Not Taken,* 17 Psychological Science 12, 1068 (2006)

Andersson, L. M., & Pearson, C. M., *Tit for tat? The spiraling effect of incivility in the Workplace,* Academy of Management Review, *24,* 452-471 (1999).

Carroll M. Brodsky, The Harassed Worker (1976)

Clive R. Boddy, *Corporate Psychopaths: Organizational Destroyers* (2011).

CPP Global Human Capital Report, June 2009.

David J. Maume, *Meet the new boss...same as the old boss? Female supervisors and subordinate career prospects,* Social Science Research Volume 40, Issue 1, January 2011)

Heinz Leymann, *Mobbing and Psychological Terror at Workplaces,* 5 Violence and Victims, 119-125 (1990).

J. Decety. et al., *Atypical empathic responses in adolescents with aggressive conduct disorder: A functional MRI investigation,* 80 Biological Psychology, Issue 2, pp. 203-211 (2009).

Jamie L. Callahan, *Incivility as an Instrument of Oppression: Exploring the Role of Power in Constructions of Civility,* Advances in Developing Human Resources 13(1) 10–21 (2011).

Joan Squelch and Robert Guthrie, *The Australian Legal Framework for Workplace Bullying*, 32 Comp. Labor Law & Pol'y Journal 15 (2010).

Joe C. Magee, et al., *"Leadership and the Psychology of Power,"* in The Psychology of Leadership: New Perspectives and Research, edited by D. M. Messick & R. Kramer (2004).

Joe C. Magee, et al., *Leadership and the psychology of power*, in D. M. Messick & R. Kramer (eds.), *The Psychology of Leadership: New Perspectives and Research* 64 (2004).

John Clarke, *Working with Monsters: How to Identify and Protect Yourself from the Workplace Psychopath* (2005).

Katherine Lippel, *Introduction*, 32 Comp. Labor Law & Pol'y Journal 2 (2010), *citing* Stale Einarsen et al., *The Concept of Bullying and Harassment at Work: The European Tradition*, in Stale Einarsen, et al, Bullying and Harassment in the Workplace: Development in Theory, Research and Practice, 3, 32 (2d ed., 2011).

Kevin M. Clermont & Stewart J. Schwab, Employment Discrimination Plaintiffs in Federal Court: From Bad to Worse? 3 Harv. L. & Pol'y Rev. 103 (2009).

Loraleigh Keashly, *Emotional Abuse in the Workplace: Conceptual and Empirical Issues*, 1 J. Emotional Abuse 85, 114 (1998).

M. Jenkins, et al., *Consequences of being accused of workplace bullying: an exploratory study*, 4 International Journal of Workplace Health Management, 33-47 (2011)

Mobbing and Emotional Abuse in the American Workplace, by Noa Zanolli Davenport PhD, Ruth Distler Schwartz, and Gail Pursell Elliott

N. Davenport, R.D. Schwartz, G.P. Elliott. *Mobbing: Emotional Abuse in the American workplace 38.* (1999).

R. Gosh, et al., *The Toxic Continuum From Incivility to Violence: What Can HRD Do?* Advances in Developing Human Resources 13(1) 3–9 (2011).

S. Lim, & L.M. Cortina, *Interpersonal mistreatment in the workplace: The interface and impact of general incivility and sexual harassment*, 90 Journal of Applied Psychology, 483-496 (2005).

Susan Stefan, *"You'd Have to Be Crazy to Work Here": Worker Stress, The Abusive Workplace, and Title I of the ADA*, 31 Loyola Los Angeles Law Review, 795, (1998).

W. Martin, et al., *What Legal Protections Do Victims of Bullies in the Workplace Have?* J. Workplace Rights, Vol. 14(2) 143-156 (2009).

World Health Organization, *Differences between normal conflicts and mobbing*, Raising Awareness of Psychological Harassment at Work, Protecting Workers Health Series No. 4 (2003). Adapted from Table No. I.

About the Author

Patricia Barnes is a judge, attorney and a recognized expert on workplace discrimination and abuse.

Ms. Barnes writes a syndicated employment law blog on discrimination, abuse and bullying called *When the Abuser Goes to Work*, http://abusergoestowork.com.

She is also the author of *Betrayed: The Legalization of Age Discrimination in the Workplace* (2014) and *Transcend Your Boss, Zen and the Difficult Workplace (2013)*. Ms. Barnes has written two books for CQ Press of Washington, DC, on the criminal justice and American court systems, respectively, and edited a three-volume series of books on domestic violence published by Garland Publishing. She has written about legal issues, including workplace bullying, for many national publications.

A resident of Reno, NV, she can be reached at barnespatg@gmail.com.

Made in United States
Orlando, FL
09 May 2025

61160904R00164